'MIRROR UP TO NATURE':
FOURTH SEAMUS HEANEY LECTURES

'MIRROR UP TO NATURE':
FOURTH SEAMUS HEANEY LECTURES

Edited by Patrick Burke

Carysfort Press

A Carysfort Press Book

'A Mirror Up to Nature': Fourth Seamus Heaney Lectures
Edited by Patrick Burke

First published as a paperback in Ireland in 2010 by
Carysfort Press Ltd
58 Woodfield
Scholarstown Road
Dublin 16
Ireland

ISBN 978-1-904505-48-8

Typeset by Carysfort Press Ltd

Printed and bound by eprint limited
Unit 35
Coolmine Industrial Estate
Dublin 15
Ireland

Cover design by Susan Meaney

This book is published with the financial assistance of
The Arts Council (An Chomhairle Ealaíon) Dublin, Ireland

Contents

Introduction: 'The Mirror up to Nature'

Between October, 2006, and June, 2007, St Patrick's College, Drumcondra, a college of Dublin City University, sponsored a programme of seven lectures on drama and theatre, under the less than totally imaginative title, *The Mirror up to Nature*. This is the fourth in the highly successful Seamus Heaney Lecture Series, inaugurated by the College and supported generously by its President, Dr Pauric Travers. They have been held biennially since 2000, each addressing themes of educational, cultural, political or artistic importance in the broad context deriving from the educational and humanities mission of the College. St Patrick's is most appreciative of the support and interest consistently shown the series by its patron, Seamus Heaney, a dedicated educator, an outstanding poet, and, be it remembered in the context of *The Mirror up to Nature*, a significant dramatist – *The Cure at Troy* (1990) and *The Burial at Thebes* (2004), versions, respectively, of Sophocles' *Philoctetes* and *Antigone*.

The content of the seven lectures is summarized below, while readers' versions of six of them are reprinted in the present volume. (Professor Ania Loomba, who spoke on drama and politics, had already pledged her contribution to another publisher.) Sadly, one of the planned lectures, to be given by that outstanding teacher, John Devitt, formerly Head of English at Mater Dei College, was overtaken by an illness which was to take him from us in June of 2007.

The first of the lectures, 'The Magic of Theatre', given by Patrick Mason, former Artistic Director of the Abbey Theatre, as well as a world-class director of drama and opera, was a *tour de force*. Drawing imaginatively on plays such as *Hecuba* and *The Winter's Tale,* their undimmed capacity to speak truth in eras of inadequate language such as our own, dominated by what he termed 'MBA man', he moved beyond mere discussion of theatre and brought us with him *into* theatre.

The occasion of the second lecture, 'The Irish Contribution' by Thomas Kilroy, was graced by the attendance of Brian Friel, whose father was an *alumnus* of the College. In characteristically penetrating style, Kilroy grounded his argument on the philosophy of the stage articulated by Yeats, his equal unease with the showiness of post-Restoration English comedy and with the visionary restrictiveness of the work of the emerging catholic nationalists such as Padraic Colum and T.C. Murray. He provocatively related that argument to the more recent work of Eugene O'Brien and Marina Carr.

Professor Ania Loomba, University of Pennsylvania, in the third lecture, spoke on the politics of drama and the drama of politics. From an initial discussion on concepts of race, nation and outsiders in some of Shakespeare's plays – Othello, Shylock – she moved on to related issues of personal and social identity both in his and later work. An impressive feature of this occasion was the lecturer's exceptional adeptness in the question-and-answer session.

At the heart of the series, reflecting the centrality of St Patrick's as a College of Education, was a pair of lectures given by two recognized world authorities in the area of drama in education. In 'The Mythic and the Mundane: the Transforming Power of Theatre and Process Drama', Professor Cecily O'Neill, stressing the primacy of imagination in education and the related importance of story and myth, argued clearly as to how they could be illuminatingly addressed through 'Process Drama', a form of drama.

Complementing that lecture in many ways was Professor Jonothan Neelands's contribution, 'Mirror, dynamo or lens? Children, drama and social change': with wit and profundity, he deployed the three images in his title (one of which, of course, he was borrowing from the overall series title) to interrogate the potential of drama in terms of photographic realism, as catalyst of social change and as vehicle of self-exploration. And so to the penultimate lecture. For over a century now, a major competitor with theatre for the attention of audiences has been film. In a wide-ranging, well-researched lecture, 'From Boucicault to Beckett: From Real to Reel (1894-2007)', Dr Brenna Katz Clarke, Head of English at St Patrick's, addressed, with characteristic *élan*, identifying dynamics of both media, supported by well-chosen film clips, notably from the marvellous *Singin' in the Rain* (dir. Kelly and Donen, 1952), a theme of which is, of course, the pivotal transition from silent to talking movies. Given her expertise in both media, it was gratifying to lovers of the stage to be informed that, if hard choices had to be made, Dr Katz Clarke's would be for drama!

The final lecture was from Dr John Buckley, Senior Lecturer in the Department of Music at St Patrick's and himself an outstanding composer. What made the occasion so memorable for those who attended was that, in addition to offering an instructive summary history of opera as an art form, Dr Buckley offered a most enlightening account of the genesis of his own opera, *The Words Upon the Window-Pane* (1991), based on Yeats's powerful play, from the introduction to which the lecture took its beautiful title, 'like a bell with many echoes: drama and opera'. The lecturer's fine discourse was complemented by the artistry of actress Imelda McDonagh, who read to fine effect some of the 'Stella' passages from Yeats's play, and that of soprano Collete McGahon, who, with assured accompaniment by Roy Holmes, sang Buckley's versions of the same passages. As a bonus, the composer's librettist, Hugh Maxton, was present. A delightful conclusion to the series.

It would be facile to suggest that what was deliberately constructed as a wide-ranging series – attempting to encompass, within a mere seven lectures, some of the many concerns of writers, theatre directors, classroom teachers, historians, experts in art forms other than drama – might issue in an accessible taxonomy of drama. Nonetheless, certain 'echoes' resonate rather more hauntingly than others from the 'bell' that was the series. One of those, uniting Patrick Mason, Cecily O'Neill, Jonothan Neelands and perhaps Ania Loomba, was the heuristic potential of drama, its power as a medium to illuminate, with unique honesty, complex considerations in philosophy, history, theology; this may be as valid for a senior infant class as for a cast embarking on Brecht's *The Life of Galileo*. Another 'echo' (in Kilroy, O'Neill, Loomba) had to do with what might be described as 'renewable tradition' – the equal importance of preserving and interrogating heritage: as our distinguished guest, Brian Friel, has Hugh, the hedge-school master, phrase it in *Translations,* while his familiar world is collapsing: 'we must never cease renewing those images [of the past] ; because once we do, we fossilize.' Professor Loomba reminded us about the ineluctable interface between a given era's construction of artistic representations and issues of *Realpolitik,* a perspective shared to a considerable extent by Jonothan Neelands. Hamlet was right on both counts – -'the play's the thing', in terms of autonomous and unique artefact, together with its moral role vis-à-vis 'the conscience of the king.'

∽∽∽

For the successful working of the series, thanks are due to the Series Committee (Dr Noreen Doody, Ms Mary Howard, Dr Marian Lyons, Ms Paula Murphy, Dr Ann O'Reilly, Dr Mary Shine Thompson, Mr Denis Twomey, Dr Alan Titley), all those who chaired lectures, especially distinguished invitees, Dr Cathy Leeney, Drama Centre, UCD, Mr Peter McDermott, DIT, Rathmines, and Professor Nicholas Grene, Chair of English, TCD; Paul Murphy and John Smith, for technological expertise, and to Raymond Topley for his skill with a camera. A special word of thanks to the unfailingly courteous and efficient College Administrator, Ms Roisin Purcell.

1 | Keeping Faith:

'It is required. You do awake your faith...'
The Winter's Tale

Patrick Mason

What's in a title?

Titles matter. The test of a good title in the commercial theatre used to be to add the proposed name to the phrase 'Could I have two tickets for...'. If the completed sentence didn't roll easily – inevitably – off the tongue ('Two tickets for Cats'; 'Two tickets for Private Lives'), the received wisdom was that you'd never sell it. Then came Dancing at Lughnasa. And although there were attempts by Broadway producers to re-entitle the play Dancin' ('Could I have two tickets for Dancin'?'), all such attempts were, thankfully, thwarted by a determined author. So, despite the desperate variations it inspired at the box office window ('Two tickets for Lugnasa; or Lugnahasy; and even, on one memorable occasion, two tickets for Lufthansa'), Dancing at Lughnasa went on to break one rule but prove another: titles are signifiers. They are pointers to meaning and theme, keys to hidden connections and symbolic significance. They are also a kindly hint by the author/playwright as to his/her larger purpose: a vain attempt to head off the inevitable misreadings of the work, – wilful or otherwise.

Three titles

This talk, which I am now presenting with some trepidation as a published lecture, has three titles: one public, one semi-public, and one private. Private, that is, until now. The semi-public title was a working title supplied by St Patrick's College when I was first invited to contribute to this series. It was 'The Glorious Heritage: Sophocles, Shakespeare, Strindberg'. This was followed closely by the public title, or rather the title used to publicize the event itself: 'The Magic that is Theatre'. The private title, which I am now using for the published account of that event, and which I omitted to reveal on the occasion, is 'Keeping Faith'. The particular faith I have in mind is that highly ambiguous faith alluded to in the final scene of Shakespeare's *The Winter's Tale*: the faith that can make a statue come to life.

So what follows is a series of reflections on three aspects of theatre: heritage, magic, and faith. As such, it was conceived as a scripted talk, something to be experienced through performance. It has proved somewhat problematic for me to adapt the energy – the emotional temperature – of that live discourse to the written page: to translate public speech into private reading. But, for better or worse, here is the attempt.

A Scheme of Sorts

Following the theme of heritage, I want to look back to the theatre of Sophocles – the Athenian Theatre and the starting point of the western theatre tradition. Following the Shakespeare/ Strindberg suggestion, I will also take a brief look at Elizabethan/Jacobean theatre and at late 19th-century theatre – social realists, symbolists, dreamers of dream plays, and so on, and leave some time and space left for a few general observations about Irish theatre, the particular branch of European theatre in which I have worked for the last 30 years. With luck, I might even manage a few insights or provocations along the way.

You will notice that I use the 'T' word. Tradition. Its replacement by the more anodyne and committee-friendly word 'heritage' is, to me, an acknowledgement that it has become a troublesome word: a word freighted with negative associations of the old, the past, the irrelevant. Living, as we do, in such a relentlessly upbeat culture, with such a perverse belief in progress, and such an unthinking bias against age and history, it would appear that 'tradition' is a word best avoided. The same could be said about 'faith', of course. Another troublesome word. So let's make double trouble, and use both.

Some Reflections on Heritage/Tradition

There is a tradition – a strong and remarkably consistent tradition – of western theatre practice from the 15th century to the present day. It is largely based on the rediscovery of ancient Roman and Greek theatre during the Renaissance: a series of readings and misreadings of Vitruvius, Seneca, Aristotle and Euripides that produced, among other things, the first opera and Revenge Tragedy. Whatever about the influence of liturgical church drama and folk drama/ritual on popular performance styles and conventions, western European theatre from the 16th century onwards has been a self-consciously 'classical' theatre. It has also been a 'poetic' theatre – some forms, such as court masque and grand opera, being notably more classical and self-consciously poetic than others.

How has this tradition been handed on? It is primarily contained in surviving play texts, libretti, and associated critical writings. It is also described in visual and written accounts of theatrical representation, in theatre's styles and conventions, and in the detailed history of theatre practice. Thirdly, there is also a large and rich store of theatrical memory amongst practitioners, past and present, a theatre lore that is both oral and written. This is a very immediate and personal manifestation of theatre tradition. Taken in conjunction with extant texts, this lore of theatre practice amplifies our knowledge of the past, fills in the missing gaps of the experience itself, as opposed to the schema of the text. It serves to remind us that we are dealing with events as well as literature – the theatrical as well as the literary.

Shakespeare was an actor before he was a poet or playwright. That was what so scandalized his contemporaries, the university poets with their Oxbridge degrees: Shakespeare didn't have the necessary qualifications to be a poet. This intellectual snobbery still goes on today, of course, with the Francis Bacon/ Earl of Oxford nonsense: he was only an actor, for God's sake, how could he have written all that stuff? There are also indications -in Athenaeus and in Plutarch – that Aeschylus, Sophocles and Euripides were actor/ directors, as well as poets. For Shakespeare and his contemporaries, one of the most startling, indeed electrifying, aspects of this re-discovery of classical theatre in the West was its non-Christian origin, its non-Christian values. The colouring of western consciousness by the rise of orthodox Christianity in the first millennium was dramatically recast by this introduction of pre-Christian pantheons and the restoration of more ancient concepts of

Fate, Necessity, Justice, and Truth by the Renaissance and, paradoxically, by the Reformation. A pre-Christian paradigm of humanness was rediscovered and, more significantly, was reanimated in the imagination of actors and audiences through the work of the public stage.

The Renaissance was the great look backwards in order to move forward – or at least to break outwards from the mindset of medieval Christendom. The Elizabethan/Jacobean playwrights looked back to Periclean Athens and the rites of Dionysus in order gain a new vision their own world – to open up a new mode of consciousness through acting out or mimesis. They called it 'personation', which term happily combined a new psychological interest in character with a powerful memory of the classical actor's 'persona' or mask.

In a similar fashion, at the end of the 19th century, Sigmund Freud and Carl Jung were to look back to the Greeks, to the myths of Oedipus and Eros, to open the way to a new mode of consciousness in the world through 'psychologizing', a move already anticipated in the later plays of Ibsen and Strindberg, among others. The creative backward look is at the heart of the European way, at the heart of European culture. But this strategy is not simply a matter of archaeology or antiquarianism. It is more a matter of creative fantasy – creating the fantasy that was Athens, the fantasy that was Rome. And at the heart of this nurturing act of willed imagination is another fantasy – the fantasy of a god: the strange imagining and re-imagining of Dionysus, the presiding deity of theatre.

Which brings us to the theme of magic, the magic in and of the theatre. For despite what we perceive as the secularizing narrative of Renaissance, Reformation, Enlightenment, and the rise of rationalism through the industrial/ scientific revolution, the theatre tradition tells another, stranger story: a narrative of moving from one manifestation to another; a narrative of a god, a root energy/ cause/ consciousness, a shaping force that acts through and on the human imagination through the medium of play: the play of Dionysus. The gods may have become our diseases, as Jung speculated, but they are still at some level our 'gods' – cultural, psychological, physical manifestations of a force or a presence that is both metaphysical and transcendental.

Some Reflections on Magic

Tradition is memory, in the fullest sense of Memoria and Mnemosyne. Memnosyne was mother of all the Muses, and so is mother of all the arts. Memoria is the culture of all cultures – the rich, nurturing soil of all imagination. For Memoria is memory as imagination, not just the faculty of recording and cognition, but a creative faculty capable of producing revelatory dreams and willed fantasies. In the western Art of Memory, this nurturing of Memoria was closely tied to the practice of theatre as the seminal works of Frances Yates suggest. Jung and Freud may have turned to the ancient theatre for the founding myths and images of their new psychological 'science', but the Renaissance poet-playwrights turned to it for the making of Soul. Another troublesome word.

The modern realm of the Soul, if there is such a thing, is now limited to a symptom of the mind, or, more minimally, a pathology of the brain. For the Greeks, and possibly for Shakespeare, it was the presence and perspective of a god inspiring the practice of an art. A healing art: an art that made whole. (Next to Dionysus the patron god of Greek theatre was Asclepius – hence the large theatre at Epidavros, built beside his sanctuary.)

But I have got ahead of myself. If not above myself! The problem with constructing grand cultural narratives is that there's an inflatus built into the process and the material that can carry you away on a current of hot air! So I will backtrack a little by talking to you about a personal experience of the tradition, and its immediate effect on me and my work. But I will return to my fantasy of the Theatre of Dionysus and its healing art before I finish.

Some Reflections on Theatre

When I stepped down from the artistic directorship of the Abbey Theatre at the end of 1999, I took a short break from theatre to recuperate and reflect on what had been an exhilarating but mixed experience. Then, in late 2000, I went back to freelance directing both here and abroad, working in opera and theatre. For those of you unfamiliar with the freelance world, I should explain that you work where you can or, at least, wherever they will have you. You also try and select the work, or influence the choices of artistic directors and intendants by pitching plays and productions that are of real interest to you and hoping they will prove sympathetic to the programmers. Earning a living is one thing – it has to be done – but it is a deadly affair when you are forced to work on any play or opera which, while feeding the body and paying the bills, is not, at some level, feeding the mind or the psyche. It is damaging to do work that does not animate.

As an Abbey Theatre artistic director I could decide to programme in a certain way and – *pace* the economics – get on with it. Now I must, like all my freelance colleagues, negotiate not only the tyranny of the box-office, the straitjacket of deficits, but also the sensibilities and tastes – social, aesthetic, political, philosophical – of administrators and curators. This can be a frustrating experience. For all our much-vaunted cult of individualism we live in an extraordinarily conformist culture, dominated by mass taste, mass marketing, and mass response – mass thinking. There are enforced orthodoxies, self-conscious trends and zeitgeists – rules of the market, rules of fashion, rules of political and cultural correctness – all imposed by various pressure groups and vested interests. These prescriptions and proscriptions weigh heavily on the choice of content of our stages. More heavily, perhaps, than we are prepared to admit.

There is also a language problem. Whatever about a traditional language of creativity, imagination, soul, the reality of working in the arts today is having to become fluent in the language of management and marketing. It is a pre-requisite of winning funding from the politicians and administrators, but also from corporate sponsors. We are all corporate now, and the global language is MBA. The big question about MBA-speak is: is this an appropriate language in which to try and talk about the working of the human imagination? Or does the language itself make it impossible to express key concepts, key values of that vital imagining process. In effect, does MBA render the soul wordless? If it can be measured, it can be managed, they assert. But do the values implicit in such a sterile system of quantification by statistical analyses distort and subvert the imaginative values of the arts by rendering them not only unsayable, but impossible to sustain? One thing is certain: the theatre culture that I trained in, and have worked in for thirty years, no longer exists. I speak a dead language.

A Crisis of Faith

To cut a longish story short, I began to run out of projects to animate me. I began to tire of the struggle to speak and think MBA. And the disastrous turn of events at the Abbey from 2000-2005 left me profoundly disillusioned and angry. I suffered a crisis of faith –

of faith in theatre. What did it have to offer me any more? What life, what real nourishment, what abundance was possible now? I had been directing for nearly thirty years, during which time I had been privileged to work with some of the very greatest Irish playwrights and actors. Thirty years that had been traduced in five. I suffered a loss of purpose – a loss of theatre soul, if you like. It was increasingly difficult to work on anything, or find anything I really wanted to work on. What to do?

I went to the theatre. Back to the Greeks.

I went to see a production of a new version of Euripides' *Hecuba* by Frank McGuinness. It was directed by Jonathan Kent at the Donmar Warehouse, London, in 2004, and starred Clare Higgins. I got on with Jonathan's production well enough, but it was not my style: too much scenery, but impressively done – and I very much admired Clare's performance: very passionate, courageous, and it well deserved the Olivier she won for it. But the play! O, my goodness – the play!

First, there was Frank's extraordinary text. Here are the opening lines:

> I am Polydorus
> Son of Hecuba,
> Priam was my father.
> I am dead.

Do you know a better opening to any play? McGuinness is at his very best: every line a lean muscle, every word a stone thrown against heart and soul. Listen to Hecuba, pleading for the assistance of Agamemnon – that exhausted pragmatist and child-killer:

> I stand here a slave, I may have no strength,
> But the gods are strong – so too is the law.
> It rules over all, mortal, immortal.
> Spit on the law, murder friends, ransack holy places,
> And if you pay no penalty or punishment
> There is no justice among men – no justice.
> But if you judge these to be acts of shame,
> Respect me, pity me, observe what I suffer.

And then there is the master playwright himself, Euripides: his extraordinary narrative, the strong characters, the savage theme, the total engagement with all that makes us human. The vividness of the storytelling, the relentless drama of its action, its intensity in performance – the breathtaking compression, the complexities, contradictions, violence, terror, irony, pathos –; and all achieved in the span of a single action lasting one hour and twenty minutes.

I knew I had to direct this play.

It so happened that, at the time, I was in discussions with Chicago Shakespeare Company about directing something for them, and I sent over a script straight away. And that's how I came to direct the American premiere of the Euripides-McGuinness *Hecuba* in Chicago, with the wonderful Marsha Mason (no relation) in the title role. And it was also how my faith in theatre was reawakened.

An Athenian epiphany, if you like – or maybe, more properly, a theophany.

All for Hecuba

The play was written at the height of the Peloponnesian war, an illegal war initiated by Athens against Sparta, and a war that proved to be the ruin of Athens and its democracy. Euripides' main source was Homer, and his setting is the aftermath of the fall of Troy. He took as his protagonist the figure of Hecuba and, with a superb disregard for geography, combined two stories concerning the fate of two of her children: the sacrifice of Polyxena, her only surviving daughter, and the murder of Polydorus, her only surviving son.

But Euripides has a third story up his sleeve. For, just when you think he has done with Hecuba's story, he links the whole action of this play back into the origins of the Troy story by taking us back to the Oresteia of Aeschylus, and forward to the blood bath that awaits Agamemnon on his homecoming. Here is the king speaking at the end of *Hecuba*:

> Hecuba, poor woman,
> Go bury your two dead bodies.
> The wind is rising to guide us.
> Safe passage to the fatherland.
> May we have peace there in our homes,
> Now that the war is over.

The women of Troy are suitably enigmatic in their final comment:

> Go to the harbours,
> Go to the tents.
> Begin our lives as slaves.
> Fate is fate.

Time bends, circles, straightens, only to bend again. Nothing is over about this war. This war is only just beginning. It is masterly playmaking. But why should it have had quite such an effect on me? Here are some notes I made at the time, in an attempt to pin down the experience and answer the question why.

Most immediately the theme: war. The world is a war. The Trojan war, of course, but with an obvious resonance – particularly here and now in America.

Women and war – Hecuba, queen and mother of Troy, her sons slaughtered, her city destroyed, being shipped back to Greece a slave in a slave transport. Women as the ultimate victims of war. The just, the righteous, pious, compassionate Hecuba – she calls herself 'the mother of all misfortunes', the other women affirm 'some god hates you'. Why such suffering? Why such terrible injustice?

Content/meaning – is meaning possible? Where is justice? Where is truth? Where are the gods, where is the law? Is there no end to this war?

The characters – narrative and theme and action effortlessly carried by character. Human beings with emotional, psychological lives – bewildered, suffering, doubting, fearing, loving, hating – trying to make sense of their lives, trying to hold on to their sanity in a world gone mad. Recognizable men and women – idealists, pragmatists, sadists, realists.

Above all a world – an imagined world complete, consistent, utterly engaging – a created world, a vessel to contain all our stories and lives: theirs and ours. So familiar, so alien, so recognizably human. Human. Inner and outer – man as the meeting of angel and animal.

Great narrative – intricate, detailed, inventive, inevitable, convincing, engaging, inescapable. A world true and entire to itself and to the characters and actions that move it along, act it out, and animate it.

The whole experience was an intense affirmation of why I had come into the theatre in the first place. Here was the action of theatre, the practice of theatre art that I believed in, that had first enthralled me. This was the magic.

The Great Globe

Which brings me to my private title for this lecture, 'Keeping Faith'. As I said at the beginning, it is a reference to the final scene of *The Winter's Tale*. 'It is required. You do awake your faith,' Paulina tells the grieving Leontes in act five, scene three, before she brings the statue of his dead wife back to life. This scene has always been a touchstone for me. It is quintessential theatre magic. The Winter's Tale is one of Shakespeare's late plays, and it is a fantasy – a fairytale. It is based on the story *Pandosto: The Triumph of Time* by his one-time rival and detractor, Robert Greene. (Greene was the man who was the model for Falstaff and Toby Belch, and who was famously carried off by a surfeit of pickled herrings – and pox, and gout, and God knows whatever other infection he picked up around Bankside.) Time is a character of the play, and the great final scene goes to the heart of his mystery and ours.

Perdita, Leontes, his daughter, and others, are in the gallery/chapel where Paulina shows them a statue of the dead queen, Hermione. She unveils the figure.

> **Leontes:** O royal piece!
> There's magic in thy majesty, which has
> My evils conjured to remembrance. And
> From thy admiring daughter took the spirits,
> Standing like stone with thee.
>
> **Perdita:** And give me leave,
> And do not say 'tis superstition, that
> I kneel and then implore her blessing.

Having whetted their appetites, Paulina offers to cover up the statue again as Leontes is becoming irrational. He wants to kiss the statue, it's so lifelike. He commands her not to cover it up. Then she makes her move.

> **Paulina:** Either forbear,
> Quit presently the chapel, or resolve you
> For more amazement. If you can behold it,
> I'll make the statue move indeed, descend,
> And take you by the hand. But then you'll think
> Which I protest against – I am assisted
> By wicked powers.
>
> **Leontes:** What you can make her do
> I am content to look on; what to speak,
> I am content to hear; for 'tis as easy
> To make her speak as move.

Paulina: It is required
You do awake your faith. Then all stand still.
Or those that think it is unlawful business
I am about, let them depart.

Leontes: Proceed.
No foot shall stir.

Paulina: Music; awake her; strike!
'Tis time. Descend. Be stone no more.
Approach.
Strike all that look upon with marvel. Come,
I'll fill your grave up. Stir. Nay, come away.
Bequeath to death your numbness, for from him
Dear life redeems you.
You perceive she stirs.
Start not her actions shall be holy as
You hear my spell is lawful. Do not shun her
Until you see her die again, for then
You kill her double. Nay, present your hand.
When she was young, you wooed her. Now in age
Is she become the suitor?

Leontes: O! she's warm!
If this be magic, let it be an art
Lawful as eating.

Polixenes: She embraces him.
She hangs about his neck.

Camillo: If she pertain to life, let her speak too.
Ay, and make it manifest where she has lived,
Or how stol'n from the dead.

Paulina: That she is living,
Were it but told you, should be hooted at
Like an old tale. But it appears she lives,
Though yet she speak not.

What is being played out here is, in effect, a play within a play of play. This is theatre that acknowledges itself as theatre to become theatre. Each layer of acknowledged illusion only serves, in performance, to make the event more real to us. Knowing it is an illusion doubles the force of illusion itself. The presence of the statue that is not a statue but is a statue, is crucial to this process. It is an 'imago', a mask, a magic door to the world within.

How is all this done? Because it appears she lives. 'Were you but told, there would be no effect, no result.' Mimesis is the key: the magic is in the acting out. It is in the presence invoked and experienced, it is the god inhabiting the persona – present through the imago/mask – in this case the actor/statue. We project onto the persona/mask and that mask, through a counterflow of imaginative energy, reflects back the contents of our fantasies; and we and the object before us are animated by the imaginary/real interaction. We enter for a brief moment that otherness that is both in us, and around us. But to experience this doubleness of being, we must first make our act of faith. In the old phrase, it requires a willing suspension of disbelief.

Look at how the playwright makes this 'suspension' so tempting and rewarding for us. He uses every narrative trick: the false starts, the pretended concern, raising the tension with warnings, misgivings ('What I am about to do...' etc.). There is the stern injunction: 'No foot shall stir'; and then, of course, music. More presence – the ultimate theatrical presence – music to animate, to redeem Time, to bring dead matter back to life. And then, more music. Shakespeare's own word music: pure spell, incantation – simple, rhythmic, hypnotic – as only he can do it. Words with music, words of music combined.

Paulina spins out this spell, plays out the tension: will the spell work? Not if we do not awake our faith, it won't. 'It is required. You do awake your faith.' There is no move at first, but then, almost imperceptibly, the first signs of life. Then the descent. The embrace. The kiss. This is conjuring of the highest order. The statue moves and we are moved with it; moved momentarily into a world of grace, a world of wholeness and of healing.

If this be magic, let it be an art lawful as eating!

The 'S' Word

I got carried away a while ago talking about Memoria, and healing, and the theatre of Dionysus. And I want to finish up by returning to that topic, and do so by way of another troublesome word: Soul. Not an inappropriate route to take, as it turns out, for one of the titles of Dionysus was Lord of Souls.

There is another motif that runs like a secret thread through all the history of theatre making – disappearing at times, reappearing at others – and it is an extremely difficult one to address in this materialistic age. It is there blatantly and excitedly in Athens; it haunts most of Shakespeare, though not all of his contemporaries. It is glimpsed in the periodic pursuit of the chimera of 'poetic drama' through the 19th and into the 20th centuries. It is there in the dream plays, the strange and sadly dated creations of the Symbolists. It is literalized in the posturing of the psychological drama – and it is squeezed out of the reductionist work of the social realists. It is a matter of faith: it is a matter of Soul. The making of Soul: the making of a new/old paradigm of humanness through the work of the imagination.

Straight Lines and Circles

If you examine the dominant MBA thought/speak of the current arts scene, you will notice that to win approval work must be adjudged 'cutting edge' and 'innovative'. There are even prestigious awards for 'risk-taking' and 'innovation' in the Arts. The entrepreneurial spirit is alive and well. No talk of remembrance, instauration (that is, renewal or repair), or of commemoration. No, we are bound by the language of MBA to technocracy and its underlying myth of Progress; the relentless, all-consuming, onward march of Progress. Whatever its benefit to the growth of the technocracy, this forced onward movement, with its deliberate denial of the past, its cultural and political amnesia, its cruel insistence that all its servants should reinvent and uproot themselves at regular intervals, its destruction of continuity, tradition, and community – this movement does enormous damage to the growth of soul.

Memoria has its own style of progression: through regression. The soul circles. The way of the Memoria is not the way of the technocracy. MBA is anathema to the process of soul-making. (And vice versa.) We can see its ill effects in the increasing obsession with form over content, style over meaning, in today's theatre. We can feel it in the reductionism of theme and matter, the flattening out of emotion and engagement, the increasingly strident taste for caricature rather than character, effect rather than experience. So often the cutting edge, the innovative, turns out, in performance, to be cartoon theatre with cartoon acting: stereotypes masquerading as archetypes. A theatre of glittering, often brilliant, surfaces that signifies – well, very little actually. A theatre perfectly suited to our dominant culture of celebrity and success, an art dedicated to prestige and prestigious awards, glib, and global.

Theatre is a communal act. We commemorate, we listen, we watch, we imagine and fantasize as part of a collective. We are present, physically at least, but also, we hope, present as consciousnesses, as psyches, to engage together in an action that is both real and actual (bound by time and space), and imaginary – part of Memoria (that is, of all time and no time, of all space and no space). And we do this for the pleasure of it, to celebrate our capacity for doing it, and to exercise this mysterious and vital faculty (What is consciousness?), and through the exercising of this faculty of soul, we can begin to nurture it and be nurtured by it, and, in the process, create more and more complete paradigms of humanness. That is why the art of theatre is so important, that is why it is so difficult. That is why it can be so rewarding. It is not just as an educational tool or a therapeutic process, though it can be used as both. It is not just propaganda, journalism, or aestheticism, though it can be used for all these purposes. It is an art because it makes us more human by insisting on the more than human – the otherness – of the life we lead; and it does so by taking us, possessing us, collectively capturing our minds and hearts – our fuller souls. Through the immediate presence of actor and action, it makes us live simultaneously in the real world and in the world of Memoria.

We should leave MBA to the technocrats, and listen more acutely, learn to respond more exactly, to the whisperings and stirrings of our human consciousness: unconscious, sub-conscious, dream, memory, fantasy. And we should remember that at the heart of our western tradition there is a god – a supra-human energy, an extraordinary nexus of madness, death, regeneration, dismemberment, remembrance: Dionysus. Athens knew him as the friendliest of all the gods to man: with his ecstatic presence, and his gifts of wine, dance, eroticism, and theatre.

The Theatre of Dionysus

I know that some, perhaps all of you will find it odd, all this talk of faith, soul, magic, gods and theatre. Many will find it alienating. Some will find it offensive. So why do I do it? I do it because it lets me talk about a presence, an effect, an energy of theatre without using the language of scientism or reducing/traducing the role of imagination in the making of theatre. Freud and Jung reached back to the Greek pantheon as reference and signifier, because it was the image and form of the Western Psyche as first experienced and first articulated. I do the same as a form of protest and redress – to protest against the stripping of soul from art, and to make redress for the reductive orthodoxies of current cultural theory. To speak of the god, you should try and speak in the language of the god. It's both a courtesy and a way of animation. To that end, I want to leave you with a final fantasy – an imagining of what a Dionysian theatre might mean for us.

A theatre sacred to Dionysus – a theatre of Dionysus – would share his characteristics, bear his marks, carry his values. It would view and express the world, and humans in the world – through his particular vision and vocabulary. He is born twice, of man and god. His nature is double. He is dismembered, only to be remembered. Again, and again. He is friendliest of the gods to man. He is a dark bull, raging. He hides in the depths – he has a home in the sea. He clings like ivy. He inspires intense collective emotions of love and rejection – he creates passionate communities. He is a god of vegetation – he is the green fuse. Regeneration, rot, germination, maturation – these are his processes. He is the circle of life, he is the life cycle. His imago or icon is the mask. He is both there, and not there. His presence and energy are channelled through the medium of his persona – the actor. He is known through performance: he is in the acting out. He is a god of comings and goings. His followers have to go out onto the mountains to sing and drum to wake him from the depths of the sea. His coming brings joy, madness, death, new life. He is known by his animals – the panther, the leopard – and by the love of women and men. Animal, erotic, bisexual, he is a protean shape-changer.

The 19th century rediscovered Dionysus as the opposite of the Apollonian as a natural force destructive to civilization. And this discovery coincides with the awakening of Dionysian theatre in the work of Ibsen and Strindberg and the dream or Symbolist movement. Jung and Freud at the some moment discovered this Lord of Psyche and renamed him Id or Unconscious (collective and individual). But the Greeks knew better. They knew that Dionysus was the dark brother of Apollo – possibly his incestuous lover. (That's what I like about the Greeks: their deep experience of human nature, unconstrained by half remembered imperatives of sin and damnation.) Dionysus is Apollo's secret brother/lover, not his opposite. They are linked. More than that: they are necessary to each other.

Every time we adopt the language of our reductive modern Apollo – the language of scientism, statistics, administration, management – we deny his dark brother. And vice versa. Every time we reduce Dionysus to a frightening communal frenzy, a senseless drumming – sensation for the sake of sensation – we lose sight of his word, his articulate, poetic, inspiring, magic word. So this strange human/inhuman force-field is not just about frenzy and carnage – although that is one manifestation of his presence, part of his affect. He has his blessing, he has his cure: he has his logos. He is a complex and complete mode of consciousness: a way of being in the world, and of expressing the world. He is his own way of revealing that world to itself by acting it out. When we start to write in his way, to act and to direct in his way – we are being Dionysian: we are being true to the basic instinct/inspiration of all western theatre. That is why, as a theatre director, I talk about him as I do, fantasize about him as I do.

Plato tells us there are three ways to soul-making, to the awakening of psyche: Love, Death and Madness. Maybe that is why this theatre of Dionysus, the Lord of Souls, circles so obsessively around these three themes: love, death, madness. But it circles, not to become addicted to the morbid or the pornographic. It circles to have life, to gain depth, to animate us more fully. It is a theatre that pitches us, through its words and actions, into a momentary experience of what it is to be fully human.

W.B. Yeats declared that the mission of his theatre, the Abbey Theatre, was to ensure that all the people should have a more intense and abundant life. He spoke, too, of the 'need to bring to the stage the deeper thoughts and emotions of Ireland'. Depth, intensity, abundance – they all seem to me essential qualities of the Dionysian theatre. The Abbey, from its foundation, stands foursquare in the great European tradition. It knows what has to be done. It has only to remember itself, and get on with the work – a work in which I very much hope to be able to participate in the future.

2 | The Irish Connection

Thomas Kilroy

Connection in theatre is made between actor and audience. Indeed, there are exemplary occasions in the theatre where you have the coming together of text, acting and audience in an experience that seems to transcend any one of the elements involved. It can only happen with great writing and great acting, of course. But my point is that in the degree of its response, the audience is testifying to the depth to which the work has penetrated its communal consciousness. In this way, audience presence or audience involvement is an essential ingredient of the theatrical experience itself. In this way, theatre, in sublime fashion, is seen in the very act of fulfilling its public function.

I will mention a few such occasions which I've experienced myself but you will have your own lists. In Ireland, Donal McCann in *Faith Healer* at the Abbey Theatre, Siobhan McKenna in *Bailegangaire* at the Taibhdhearc in Galway. I would add three productions from outside Ireland from the fifties and sixties, Laurence Olivier in *The Entertainer* at the Royal Court in London, Uta Hagen in *Who's Afraid of Virginia Woolf?* in New York and Jean-Louis Barrault in *La Tentation de Saint Antoine* at the Odeon in Paris. All of these performances had a profound connection to the local culture. They tapped into some particular, native, shared experience, opening an unhealed wound, as it were, stirring a brew that had been dormant, bringing to the surface something familiar but unacknowledged in quite this public way before. They spoke not only to the audience but they also spoke for the audience. The audience provided a rippling, potent presence as part of the theatrical event.

What is interesting, and of some relevance to my topic, is that such a theatrical experience on home ground and that abroad, may have slightly different perspectives. At home one is fully part of the audience, surrendering to that tunnelling down into the communal consciousness. Abroad, there may be that too but there is also some degree of remove, of observing the audience as a visitor and saying, yes, this is what it must mean to them.

All of this has to do with the way theatre relies upon the familiar but transforms it, making it new, fresh, even strange and outlandish in that journey up on the stage and through the individual vision of the writer. The familiar in a play is likely to embrace the social, political background of the country, in a way offering a version of history. The familiar, too, is to be found in the language used. But if it is a demon-stration of the language of the people, it is a demonstration of that language stretched to some limit of its capability.

To take such exceptional events is one way of starting a discussion about the characteristic theatre of any one country. Why is it that some dramatic actions are more meaningful than others to more people in a given community? What does the characteristic performance tell us about Irish theatre? And how does it translate the local experience for a non-Irish audience?

I thought maybe this is the approach I should take this evening. In the end I decided to go a different way. But I do want to hang this picture of the exemplary theatrical event in front of me as I proceed, as a kind of corrective perhaps to what I have to say.

What I will do instead is return to the hoary old question of tradition and I hope those of you who have heard me rattling on about this in the past will bear with me. I want to use this to reflect upon the way tradition has both released and inhibited the Irish stage. And I want to end by looking at a number of plays by young Irish playwrights today, asking in what way do they reflect that tradition gone before. In doing this I will come back to the actor.

Fourteen years ago in the *Irish University Review* I wrote about the trifurcated tradition of Irish drama in the English language. When I was invited to give this talk I was asked to go back to that essay and try to expand on it in the light of more recent Irish theatre. The trifurcation that I was talking about there was, firstly, the fracture between the theatre of Anglo-Irish playwrights of the seventeenth, eighteenth and nineteenth centuries and the theatre established by Yeats and his contemporaries. Then there was the fracture between the theatre of Yeats and that of our theatre of the second half of the twentieth century. Three very different bodies of drama, then, by playwrights born on this island.

The question here is what continuity exists between these three areas of dramatic writing by Irish-born playwrights in the English language, from the seventeenth up to the second half of the last century? The answer has to be: very little indeed. Nor, given the history of the island over that period, is this particularly surprising.

I do want to remark, however, on two legacies received by playwrights of my generation from the Anglo-Irish drama of the past, one having to do with value and one with genre.

The first is the transmission of certain values about playwriting, the most important of which is the idea that drama can attain to the quality of literature. Intrinsic to this is the pre-eminence of verbal language in a play, the theatricalizing of vernacular speech, allied to a highly developed consciousness of form in the writing, including an allusive-ness, a referential mode in the writing where plays feed upon other plays as well as other kinds of writing.

In genre, there is the legacy of the peasant play from the theatre of Yeats and his contemporaries, one of the most durable forms of drama in modern Irish theatre. The peasant play of Yeats's theatre was written by Anglo-Irish playwrights who were separated from their peasant material, outsiders writing about a world that was, in ethos, removed from them, politically, socially, and culturally.

Their choice of subject, then, was deliberate, a self-conscious choice based upon a late Romantic idea of the authenticity of the natural man close to the soil. This turning to life on the periphery of the centre is a feature of some modernist art, a kind of neo-primitivism. It is as if an over-ripe, over-sated central culture had this need to strip away the inessential and find in a simpler society some human qualities lost through sophistication.

For Yeats, Synge and Gregory, with their deep interest in ancient Gaelic saga material, there was a further bonus. The Irish peasant, through folklore and story telling, seemed a living embodiment of this great literary tradition of the Irish sagas, otherwise available only in translation and in libraries. In other words there was the exciting discovery that the great mythic tales existed in two forms, the formal, written one and the vernacular one of oral story telling. This latter was a considerable stimulus to the writing of the new drama.

Synge's highly individualistic vision took all this a stage further. His vision as an artist was based upon a secular spirituality and an almost monkish, personal pursuit of dispossession, a divesting of material things and, obviously, of the comforts of his own, middle-class, Anglo-Irish background. He was drawn to extreme poverty as a testing ground of reality, as, indeed, was Beckett following after him. The idea that truth may be found more readily on the margins of existence, among the deprived and dispossessed should sit uneasily in an age of consumerism, celebrity and technological progress. However, as I've been suggesting, modernity has always sought out such a retreat in art, perhaps out of escape, perhaps as a way of flattering its own culture's tolerance. The Irish peasant play is part of this.

When, after Synge's death, Irish playwrights of actual rural background emerged, a different kind of peasant play emerged with them. This new drama was based upon intimate knowledge of the material and, in many instances, a realistic portrayal of rural society. With the change from an agricultural economy to one based upon technology, with the rapid disappearance of the family farm, the very material of this kind of play has become extinct. The playwrights, too, have exhausted the genre, in very different ways, in plays like *Translations*, *Bailegangaire* and *The Field*. Such a pervasive form of drama often ends in self-conscious parody, particularly when the material itself has begun to disappear and so, perhaps, its final manifestation is to be found in the parodic comedy of Martin McDonagh.

This point is well made by Michael Cadden in a recent issue of the Princeton University Library Chronicle devoted to Irish drama. He says McDonagh's work 'seems wilfully perverse when read in relation to the great tradition it to some degree mimics and to some degree takes the mick out of – a perversity that can be seen as an act of violence aimed at the hegemony enjoyed by the Western play in the canon of Irish literature'. McDonagh, he elaborates, 'seems to both use and abuse the form of peasant drama'.

At any rate, these legacies of literary drama and of the peasant play have steered our theatre in a particular direction affecting the characteristic style, not only of our writing of plays, but of our acting and productions as well.

I, for one, see this direction as one of enormous richness. But I also see how it has inhibited the development of other kinds of theatricality, the theatre of other languages of the human body other than the verbal. The language of image-making, of movement, and of the dynamic between the human figure in a decorated stage space has only become a prominent one in our theatre in recent years.

The pivotal figure in all this discussion is Yeats. He understood the separation of his theatre from that of his Anglo-Irish predecessors like Sheridan and Goldsmith or even contemporaries, like Wilde and Shaw. He also saw the way in which younger Catholic playwrights, like Padraic Colum and T.C. Murray, were producing a type of play that was markedly different to that of himself and of his Anglo-Irish contemporaries.

Yeats is also the Irish theorist who most effectively described the nature of literary drama. The key here is the dramatist's use of language. Dramatists who infuse language with a highly developed personal vision may create literature. Dramatists who simply record the language of the street or the market place will not. Yeats here is thinking of the naturalistic drama of someone like Ibsen or Shaw. But it also reflects his distaste for younger Catholic playwrights of peasant plays, like Padraic Colum, who were bringing a new naturalistic drama into his own theatre. Here he is on the subject:

> If one has not fine construction. one has not drama, but if one has not beautiful or powerful and individual speech, one has not literature, or, at any rate, one has not great literature. Rabelais, Villon, Shakespeare, William Blake would have recognized one another by their speech. It is only the writers of our modern dramatic movement, our scientific dramatists, our naturalists of the stage, who have thought it possible to be like the greatest and yet to cast aside the poor persiflage of the comedians, and to write in the impersonal language that has come, not out of individual life, nor out of life itself, but out of the necessities of commerce, Parliament, of Board Schools, of hurried journeys by rail.

When Yeats came to set up his own theatre he had to remove himself and his endeavours from those of his great Anglo-Irish predecessors in the theatre. As a young man striving to create a new Irish literature in the English language he did look to his Anglo-Irish heritage but not to the dramatists. He looked, rather, to other poets like Davis and Ferguson who, like himself, had drawn from native Irish material or to popularizers of such material such as Standish Hayes O'Grady, all precursors, in other words, of himself. To find out what he thought of Anglo-Irish playwrights like Farquahar, Goldsmith and the others I'll just give two examples.

In 1895 Yeats was busy defining the canon of Irish literature during the course of which he engaged in debate with Professor Edward Dowden of Trinity College. Dowden had offered his own additions to this ideal library of Irish books and he included the plays of Farquhar, Goldsmith and Sheridan. Yeats would have none of this. He said the professor knew nothing of Irish literature and, worse, had 'set himself upon the side of academic tradition in that eternal war which it wages on the creative spirit'.

In 1904 Yeats returned to the topic of an Irish canon in a public dispute with the English journalist Clement Shorter who was also a friend. Yeats had praised Lady Gregory's *Cuchulain of Muirthemne* 'as the best book that has come out of Ireland in my time'. In his response Shorter referred to 'the many great writers' of the 'past of whom England and Ireland may be equally proud'. Among these he included Goldsmith and Sheridan. Yeats's extraordinary reply to this was that the eighteenth century Anglo-Irish playwrights 'hardly seem to me to have come out of Ireland at all'.

An older Yeats was to re-embrace his Anglo-Irish heritage. But even then he did not turn to the witty writers of the Comedy of Manners. Instead he turned to Swift, Berkeley and Burke more as iconic representatives of a threatened culture than as individual writers or philosophers or political theorists. The Anglo-Irish playwrights could never fulfill this function for Yeats.

With regard to his great Anglo-Irish theatrical contemporaries, Wilde and Shaw, who had turned to the English stage and English audiences, Yeats is on record in 1902 as having said that they were the only playwrights of the nineteenth century 'worth going to hear'. The emphasis on the aural is telling. It would be impossible in a short space to convey the complexity of Yeats's relationship to either man. With Wilde it involved great personal loyalty on the part of Yeats as well as the incorporation of Wilde by Yeats, as an important symbolic figure, into his reading of history, but Yeats was never enthusiastic about Wildean theatre.

With Shaw, Yeats had a life-long engagement, never entirely easeful but it did involve sponsorship of Shaw's work and support of Shaw in his fight against English stage censorship. Nevertheless, at the end of the day, Yeats assigned both Wilde and Shaw to a state of rootlessness, men suspended between two cultures, the English and the Irish, 'abstract, isolated minds', as he put it in one of the commentaries in *The King of the Great Clock Tower*, 'without a memory or a landscape'. This marks a significant breach, then, in Anglo-Irish culture which had to do with the anchorage, rootedness within native Irish tradition on his part and the absence of it in the theatre of Goldsmith or Wilde.

When he looked at the newly emerging playwrights of the next generation, not from his own Anglo-Irish background but from Catholic Ireland, Yeats was even more disenchanted. After Synge's death in 1907 he came to realize that the theatre which he had nurtured with Gregory and Synge had been taken over by a new, naturalistic drama. He hated this naturalism in theatre which he associated with an impoverished mind, with writers who had no freedom from their subject matter, who were, so to speak, overwhelmed by sociology. There is little doubt that he considered such work as lacking in literary quality. Here is how he put it in one of his more intemperate moods:

> I have noted by the by that writers in this country who come from the mass of the people – or, no, I should say from Catholic Ireland have more reason than fantasy. It is the other way with those who come from the leisured classes. (Yeats means the Anglo-Irish) They stand above their subject and play with it and their writing is, as it were, a victory as well as a creation. The others – Colum and Edward Martyn for instance – are dominated by their subject, with the result that their work as a whole lacks beauty of shape, the organic quality.

In other words, the quality of literature. I should now say that this idea of drama as literary text is not a universally accepted one of what a play should be. If the decade 1899-1909 is the one which established the primacy of text in the Irish theatre it is also the decade when Adolph Appia's developing ideas about staging and the early work of Gordon Craig were shifting theatre away from the word to design, lighting, music and the dynamic between the human body and the space it occupies, those other mysterious languages of theatre.

Yeats admired Craig's design from the beginning but it was not until after Synge's death, from 1909 to 1912, that the two men collaborated, with Craig's screens at the Abbey and Yeats's revising of earlier plays to stage them in this highly visual form of theatre. It was only then than Yeats gave himself fully to the eurhythmic, the plastic, the physicality of the stage and in this way re-entered the modern theatre but from a different angle. At a personal level, this is the Yeats, the playwright, that I have most interest in.

I'm now going to shift tack completely and, at the risk of over-generalizing, I'm going to comment upon a number of new plays by young Irish playwrights, in the light of what I've been talking about. These plays are to be found in John Fairleigh's recent anthology *The Tiger in Winter: Six Contemporary Irish Plays..*

In Mark Doherty's impressive play *Trad* you have a father and son wandering about on a journey towards death. One of the recurring motifs in the bleakly comic exchanges between the father, Da, and his son, is precisely the subject of tradition. But it is tradition bled of all its weight, all its substance, a post-traditional treatment of tradition, where tradition has now become an item of comic indignation, an item of stand-up comedy.

Son: (*exploding*)

Ahhhhhhhhh! What is it that you want ...? Da ...? What is this tradition thing that gives you all your energy? Hah ...? Your great-great-grandchildren telling the same stories that you're telling me now? Is that it? Is that what you want? Is that what tradition is? Everyone standing still and facing backwards?

In this play, father and son scramble across a stage littered with the props of the Irish peasant play, a cottage interior, a field, a graveyard, stone walls. There is even Synge's ravenous sea at the end. But that's all they are, props. There is no grounding in a reality beyond the stage. We've gone past that requirement. The journey of the two is on a stage, the location is stage space. References to landscape invite one even further into artifice, rather than to reflection on the real thing. An allusion to Vladimir and Estragon is inescapable, (there are even two encounters with others on this journey). This is sophisticated, parodic writing of a contemporary kind.

Two young Irishmen working for the summer in the Canadian tobacco fields is the unusual setting of Malachy McKenna's *Tillsonburg*. A young couple pour out their hearts to the audience in Eugene O'Brien's *Eden*, a shocking, poignant play about small town life in the Midlands. Christian O'Reilly's *The Good Father* has a young woman and a young man meeting and remeeting and meeting again in a wryly comic sexual twosome. In Gerald Murphy's *Take Me Away* a father and three sons engage in a savage, emotional strip session, as they plan a visit to an absent mother, a visit that never takes place. The turbulent life of the snooker-player Alex Higgins is portrayed in Richard Dormer's *Hurricane*. These plays are by male playwrights. But if you were to include Stella Feehily's vivid play *Duck*, for instance, about two young drifting Dublin women, the generalizations that I'm going to make would still apply.

There is no question about the quality of the writing in these plays, some of it is of very high order indeed. What is remarkable, however, is the extraordinary resilience of social naturalism in these works, the naturalism that Yeats railed against. But these plays do not suffer from the playwrights being dominated by their subject matter, as Yeats put it. Quite the contrary, here you have a very self-confident control over the material.

The world conjured up in these plays, one shared across virtually all of them, is a world in which the old-fashioned codes of behaviour, the rituals which once made social encounters bearable, have withered away. There is no reserve here, any more, the action seems unmediated, offered just as it is. Every contact is intense, immediate and frontal, sometimes violently so. Encounters become collisions.

Nor are these large-scale works, using all the resources of the modern stage. All have small casts. Even when the action roams the pervasive sense is of confinement. Everything is directed inwards towards closely observed detail. The rhythm is often driven through duologues, in exchanges that are wound-up to extreme limits and then cut loose. This extreme effect is found also in Eugene O'Brien's play *Eden*, even though the man and woman are separated through monologue. All of this fits the common theme across all the plays, human need, need of sex, of course, although love is in short supply, but sometimes just an unappeasable, almost inexpressible need for an inexpressible goal.

It may be significant that at least five of the seven playwrights mentioned here come to playwrighting out of acting. Certainly, these plays are very much actor-vehicles. Returning to the point with which I began, contemporary Irish drama is dominated by the figure of the actor. There is little room here for directorial flourishes. Instead you have some brilliantly constructed moments for Irish acting, depending upon the old staples of the school, closely observed characterization, a wicked ear for the vernacular and a sense of timing in that comedy of desperation which has been such a feature of Irish drama over the decades.

If I see any one figure behind these plays, a presiding presence, as it were, it would be Tom Murphy. The Tom Murphy of *A Whistle in the Dark* or *Conversations on a Homecoming*, for example, who excavated Irish family life with such ferocity, particularly through the rituals of Irish male lives. Having seen Stuart Carolan's *The Empress of India*, I feel the other Murphy, the visionary, mystical Murphy of plays like *The Sanctuary Lamp* and *Too Late for Logic*, may also be influencing young Irish playwrights. Connection, then. It may not be quite one of the connections with which I started this talk but it is still a connection.

3 | The Mythic and the Mundane: the transforming power of Theatre and Process Drama

Cecily O'Neill

This paper reflects on the transforming power of drama and theatre, the significance of imagination in the curriculum and the importance of our cultural heritage in sustaining our sense of ourselves in the Ireland of the 21st century.

In his poem 'Real Names', dedicated to his friend the playwright Brian Friel, Seamus Heaney recalls school productions of Shakespeare and the transformations wrought upon his schoolfellows:

> Enter Owen Kelly, loping and gowling,
> His underlip and lower jaw ill-set,
> A mad turn in his eye, his shot-putter's
> Neck and shoulders still a schoolboy's.
> I won't forget his Sperrins Caliban,
> His bag-aproned, potato-gatherer's Shakespeare:
> And I with my long nails will dig thee pig-nuts.
> Who played Miranda?
> Some junior-final day-boy.
> Flaxen, credible, incredible
> In a braided wig and costume, speaking high,
> He was a she angelic in the light
> We couldn't take our eyes off.
> House lights down,
> Liam McLelland enters, Ferdinand
> Sleepwalking to the music, spied upon

By Gerry O'Neill cloaked up as Prospero...
The previous year
Gerry had been Macbeth, green football socks
Cross-gartered to his Thane of Cawdor knees...

In Heaney's poem the boys are transformed as they take on these great roles – Caliban, Miranda, Prospero, Macbeth – but at the same time they remain obviously schoolboys in green football socks. Through the transforming power of theatre there is a kind of double vision at work. The spectators engage in an imaginative conspiracy that allows them to see the players as Shakespeare's characters and at the same time the schoolboys they really are. As Heaney recognizes, a chink opens 'upon a scene foreseen and enterable'.[1] Process Drama engages the participants in a similar conspiracy. Like theatre, it is a mode of dramatic activity that allows entry to those 'foreseen and enterable scenes', so that spectators and participants can explore their unacted parts and unlived lives. Children also engage in this conspiracy in their own play, or at least they used to. As Yeats knew, 'Children play at being great and wonderful people, at the ambitions they will put away for one reason or another before they grow into ordinary men and women.[2] I once asked a ten-year old boy why he thought I never asked the class to pretend to be children in the drama. He said: 'It's obvious. We know how to be children. We need practice in being grown-up'. The best play, like much of the best theatre, is small-scale in extent but unlimited in its ambitions.

Theatre and Process Drama rely on an ability to pretend. Actors, audience and participants all pretend that the fictional world they are engaged in has some reality. It's worth remembering that 'to pretend' has another meaning – it means to aspire to something, to have pretensions beyond the actual state of events. Involvement in dramatic play and in Process Drama turns children into young pretenders as they take on imaginary roles and situations. This pretending may give them a sense of their own potential and encourage their aspirations as they create imaginary worlds, and project into virtual lives.

All dramatic activity and indeed engagement with any of the arts demands the use of our imaginations. Imagination is behind all the great things that have been said and done in the world. The greatest discoveries, all the greatest reforms, have all been imagined first. Not a poem has been written, not an idea developed, not an invention perfected that has not first been imagined. Every intellectual activity arises from the power of the imagination, as Einstein acknowledged.

In many of our schools it is as if the educators are determined to root out this essential but problematic human attribute. Discussion and debate are discouraged, creativity withers, questions always have a right answer and the points system reigns supreme. But we shouldn't forget that true education in any discipline is never just a collection of facts and skills. Education implies that one's outlook is transformed by what one knows, so that one learns to see, to experience the world in a new way. As Lady Gregory reminded students at the University of Pennsylvania in 1912, education is what you remember when you've forgotten what you've learned.

How do we develop this indispensable human attribute in our teachers and children? Learning how to engage the imagination should have a central place in teacher-preparation programmes. It's been claimed that teaching is storytelling and that lessons should be organized to recognize this principle – and not just in the humanities. Some of the most significant stories of our contemporary culture are expressed in science and mathematics.[3] Whatever the subject, every teacher should aim to be a successful storyteller. Research has shown that one of the keys to literacy development is consistent exposure to storytelling in both home and school environments. Stories provide basic training for the imagination. Storytelling is the easiest way to nurture imagination and that has been the basis of human learning for millennia. There should be space in the curriculum for children to listen to stories and for teachers to discover how to tell stories effectively.

The story is a cultural universal – everyone in every culture has told and enjoyed stories – stories which frequently share the same themes and motifs. As the poet, Ted Hughes puts it, they are as alike as the lines on the palm of the human hand.[4] Consider, for example, Heaney's re-telling of the *Seal Wife Myth* in his poem 'Maighdean Mara'.[5] This wonderful tale of transgression and transformation is essentially the same story as countless others around the world. In the South Seas the wife is really a dolphin. She is a goose in Canada and a crane in Japan. And in each story comes the bleak ending – 'ni thanagh Mamai ar ais aris.' The more we come to know these great stories, myths and legends from all the world's cultures, including our own, the more of ourselves and the more of the world is revealed.

Storytelling has an even older place in Irish culture than drama, and it was on our own myths, folk tales and stories from history that the founders of our National Theatre based their work. Yeats insisted that 'each fountain of story was 'a new intoxication for the imagination of the world', and believed that storytellers exist to remind us of what we might have been.[6] Legends and folk-tales were, for him, the greatest treasures the past has handed down to us. He wrote:

> It is easier to believe that times and seasons change than that imagination and intellect change; for imagination and intellect are that which is eternal crying out against that which is temporal and perishing.

For Yeats, the only game worth the labour was the creation of what he called 'a great community'. He felt that the way to do this was to create 'the old foundations of life'.[7] What are these old foundations of Irish Life and are they still relevant in the Ireland of the 21st century? Which are the 'primary ideas' on which we can base a sense of ourselves? What is most worth preserving in our heritage? Which traditions will serve us best? And in our fast-changing world how can we know what will be worth teaching and learning in twenty years time? Perhaps if we remember what we value about our country and our culture, and build on our complex past we'll be better placed to create a viable future in a world that is increasingly diverse in many ways and in others depressingly homogenous. I'm not arguing for a return to insularity. That would be impossible – Ireland, like every other nation in this century, is open to the four winds of the world. After all, 'If we do not know the best that has been said and written in the world, we do not even know ourselves.'[8]

When we recognize and accept our own cultural heritage we may be in a position to understand the culture of others – and to welcome encounters with their stories, legends, and works of art. Every nation's sense of itself is necessarily bound up with its understanding of its own cultural traditions. Vaughan Williams insisted that 'Without local loyalty there can be nothing for the wider issues to build on.'

Our greatest writers past and present knew the importance of local loyalty as a foundation for wider issues. In the lectures she gave to American audiences, Lady Gregory was fond of quoting Turgenev –'Without nationality there is no art, nor truth, nor life, nor anything.' She argued for a wise parochialism, which is very different to nationalism:

> The object of my heart is the making of the soul of Ireland sacred by getting legends known. By translating a legend or some piece of folklore we may give the hills and fields a new meaning, a new inspiration – thus bringing back the soul of Ireland to herself.[9]

Yeats agreed that legends and folk-tales were the greatest treasures the past has handed down to us. He claimed that 'A strong wind blows from the ancient legends of Ireland.'[10] The best of our contemporary playwrights may have felt the breath of this wind – *Dancing at Lughnasa*, among other plays, imagines the impact of ancient tradition on 20th century life. A powerful sense of nationality and locality underpins the work of many Irish dramatists, yet the international success of their plays indicates that they are in no sense merely parochial. They place their work in precise locations, both actual and fictional – think of Friel's fictional Ballybeg, or McDonagh's use of Leenane and Inishmann, or McPherson's Dublin of *Shining City*, or Carr's *By the Bog of Cats...* They all share a profound delight in language and the power of words, a belief in the importance of a sense of place, and an ability to connect their work with the tales and traditions of their own culture.

An important characteristic that distinguishes the creations of our greatest writers, including Seamus Heaney, is the way in which they unite the mythic and numinous with the local and the mundane. One of the most recent examples in my experience is Conor McPherson's *The Seafarer* where, during a drunken Christmas Eve in Dublin, a modern manifestation of Mephistopheles arrives to claim the soul of one of the characters. The Abbey founders were well aware of the power of a sense of place and the significance of giving their characters 'a local habitation and a name.' Although Finn McCool may have had the blood of the gods in his veins, when Lady Gregory was collecting local folk tales near her home in Coole Park, she was informed on good authority that 'Finn was the son of an O'Shaughnessy who lived at Kiltartan Cross'. (Gregory, 1904) The local people had claimed this mythic figure for one of their own. He was established in a network of local relationships, making him at once both lesser and greater than the Finn Mc Cool of legend.

I encountered this same blurring of the boundaries between ancient legend and contemporary life a couple of years ago. As part of a research project organized by the Abbey's Education and Outreach department, I was observing a class in a primary school outside Dublin. Working with a theatre director, the children had set up the Castle of Finn McCool in the school hall. They had become the inhabitants – servants, cooks, warriors. They had enacted a battle with a dragon and held a banquet to celebrate Finn's victory over the fearsome creature.

At the end of the session I asked if I could join in, and knocked at the castle gates – two benches – looking for food and shelter. I told them I'd heard about the great battle with the dragon and the children offered me the remains of the imaginary feast. As I pretended to eat, I asked what they'd done with the dragon's carcass. 'We cooked it', announced one of Finn's cooks. 'You're eating it'. I was horrified. 'Don't you know the legend?' I asked. 'Don't you know what's going to happen to me now?' 'Oh yes', said the cook, 'You'll turn into a dragon as well. Look, it's happening already. You're getting all scales.'

My hands began to curve into claws. 'Help me' I begged, 'Is there nothing I can do?' 'You'll have to go to Knock', announced one of the boys, a traveller, who'd decided he was Finn. 'But there's no time – it's happening too fast!' 'Wait', he said, 'I've got some holy water from Knock'. He sprinkled me with pretend holy water, and I was saved. I was fascinated by this seamless integration of the mythic and the everyday, the pre-Christian and the Christian, in this short interchange.

This improvised dramatic exchange had some of the characteristics of Process Drama. (O'Neill, 1995) Process Drama is almost synonymous with the term 'drama in education' but stresses the fact that it is the process of engagement in the experience that is central. Although some of the elements of the experience may be prepared or rehearsed, there is no expectation that the work will result in a performance to an audience. Instead, its purpose is to generate a dramatic elsewhere, a fictional world which may yield new insights, understandings and interpretations of the subject matter.

Other characteristics of Process Drama include the following:

- It doesn't depend on a script or a pre-determined scenario, although it may be based on existing stories or texts.

- It extends over time, and is built up from a series of episodes. These may be improvised or prepared.
- The whole group of participants is engaged in exploring the same thematic material.
- There is no external audience, but participants are an audience to their own explorations.
- Multiple perspectives and different ways of seeing the world are celebrated; problems may have more than one solution, or none, and questions more than one answer; above all, the participants' perceptions, interpretations and imaginings will be accepted and honoured. It is essentially a social event, one that depends on debate and dialogue.

Of course this kind of work is only one of the ways in which children may engage in dramatic activity. The experience of theatre – reading dramatic texts, watching plays and taking part in performances in schools or youth theatres will all be highly significant in developing children's understanding of the power of drama. The effectiveness of Process Drama lies in its invitation to an active and immediate participation in the worlds of text, of story, of history. There is cultural enrichment as the work connects with myth and history and literature and science as well as all the other materials of the curriculum. There is an enlargement of experience as children's imaginations are projected into other situations, other times and other 'foreseen and enterable' lives.

The founders of our National Theatre believed passionately in the power of theatre to educate and transform – not just a class of children, but the sensibilities of a nation. They knew that their purposes would not be achieved by a narrow didacticism, or a limited propagandist agenda, but through delight in the power of story and the seduction of language. They understood that the greatest playwrights and storytellers never try to teach direct lessons or deliver homilies. Instead these artists raise questions, create dilemmas and unsettle us so that our comfortable moral, social and political values are challenged.

Lady Gregory was particularly aware of the potential of theatre to enrich and extend children's understanding. She knew that a wise education should begin by cherishing what is already in the minds of children rather than by giving them barren knowledge of far-off places and events. The idea that Process Drama could be a source of knowledge and insight within the curriculum would certainly not be strange to her. She had a vision of what sounds like an early version of a Theatre in Education company. In notes for a lecture she gave in the United States she wrote:

> It is my dream that some day there may be a company of players getting enough support to go from county to county and from barony to barony with historical plays only, and that all our history may be shown little by little by one writer or another in the flashlight of the stage.

I'm intrigued that she uses a flashlight as a metaphor. It's not a searchlight – it illuminates only a small area. It has a tight focus. It is an individual item, a personal tool. Sometimes the batteries fail, and the light is weak and fitful. But a flashlight helps us to find our way through the dark to the light of understanding. She would be impressed with the work of Ireland's Theatre in Education companies, Team in Dublin, and Graffiti in Cork. She would have been fascinated by the developments in drama education, and the work of companies dedicated to presenting theatre for young audiences. The outstanding achievements of the Ark Cultural Centre for Children would have impressed and delighted her.

Both theatre and drama should be 'wise disturbers of the peace'.[11] But this may not recommend drama to the teacher who fears an undisciplined classroom when debate and dialogue are encouraged. Actually I wonder whether teachers really fear that they'll lose physical control of their classes. Perhaps underlying their fears is the thought that new ideas might possibly come into the classroom – ideas that might disturb the peace, notions that they might have to validate and respond to or, indeed, that the children might actually have fun. But we shouldn't forget that interest and enjoyment are always the most powerful sources of discipline.

There are many encouraging signs that bode well for the future of drama in Irish education. One is the new primary drama curriculum. Another is the publication of books that expressly address the new curriculum in a specifically Irish context. Two recent examples are *Discovering Drama* by Paula Murphy and Margaret O'Keefe, and *Step by Step* by Sarah Fitzgibbon and Joanna Parkes. Both of these very helpful books will give teachers the confidence to begin this work. Another important element is the tremendous energy and success of the Youth Theatre movement in Ireland. Several playwrights who have begun by writing for youth theatres have gone on to distinguish themselves in mainstream theatre. An English theatre director told me recently that he believed Youth Theatre was where true innovation and experiment was happening in Irish theatre, not in the subsidized companies. The National Association for Youth Drama publishes an outstanding journal that convincingly demonstrates the range and quality of the work.

A recent development is the effort of the Arts Council of Ireland to connect the work of artists and arts organizations with the requirements of formal education. Visiting artists and the involvement of arts organizations in school can be a real source of enrichment for teachers and children. There has been a similar development in the UK with the implementation of the Creative Partnerships scheme.[12] The scheme works best when it really is a partnership – when visiting artists and arts organizations are not merely invited to deploy their own skills in schools, but actively to recruit and build on the expertise of the teacher. Instead of being side-lined and disempowered, teachers should be included as co-artists, able to bring their own teaching skills and their own creativity to the work. Only sustained collaboration will actually produce positive growth. Research has shown, time and again, that real as opposed to cosmetic changes in the culture of a school or in the curriculum have to begin with the teacher. Unless the teacher changes, nothing changes.

But those of us who are teachers must not leave it to others, however skilled, to provide the imaginative life of our classrooms – we must take responsibility ourselves for promoting active engagement and encouraging imagination, those 'wings growing in the mind', in Wordsworth's phrase. Instead of being content to remain 'transmission devices', we can become 'human events'. [13] We know that drama and the other arts have the power to transform classrooms into places where something happens. Progress may be slow at first, and efforts may be dogged by frustration and failure. But we mustn't fall into lamentation mode, or make the huge mistake of doing nothing because we can only do a little.

Providing the kind of education in drama and the arts that activates imagination and resourcing and supporting the teachers will always be expensive, but think for a moment what ignorance costs us. When our children leave school, the various subjects of the curriculum may play a very small part in their lives. But they are all likely to form friendships and relationships, make decisions, take jobs and rear children. We are expected, as parents and educators, to give our children the skills and knowledge to cope with the material demands of society. But we have other responsibilities.

We should aim to give them access to the resources of their imaginations, as well as an understanding of their cultural heritage. We should try to introduce them to the treasury of the world's stories and literature and ideas; we should help them to understand their own feelings and those of others; we should develop their moral capacity; we should give them a glimpse of the kinds of social roles available to them; we should help them gain a sense of community. If we do none of these things then our children, however comfortable their material circumstances may be, are likely to approach their adult lives impoverished and disadvantaged in ways it is unlikely that any social or political remedy will be able to alleviate.

Bibliography

Bruner, Jerome, *Actual Minds, Possible Worlds* (Cambridge, Mass.: Harvard University Press, 1986).

Banaji, S, Burn, A and Buckingham *The Rhetorics of Creativity: A review of the Literature* (London: The Arts Council, 2006).

Egan, Kieran, *Teaching as Storytelling* (Chicago: Chicago University Press, 1989).

Fitzgibbon, S. and J. Parkes, *Step by Step* (Dublin: NAYD, 2006).

Gregory, Lady, *Gods and Fighting* Men (London: John Murray, 1904).

---, Notes from a lecture, undated. Lady Gregory Papers, Berg Collection, NY Public Library.

---, *Our Irish Theatre. A Chapter of Autobiography* (Gerrards Cross: Colin Smythe, 1913).

Heaney, Seamus, 'Maighdean Mara', in *Wintering Out* (London: Faber and Faber, 1972).

---, 'The Real Names', in *Electric Light* (London: Faber and Faber, 2001).

Henderson, Michael, 'Mozart could tame the savage beasts', in *The Daily Telegraph*, 20.1.2007.

Hughes, Ted, in *The Symbolic Order*, ed. Peter Abbs (London: Routledge, 1989).

Murphy, P. and M. O'Keefe, *Discovering Drama* (Dublin: Gill & Macmillan Ltd, 2006).

Yeats, W.B. Preface to *Gods and Fighting Men*, by Lady Gregory (London, John Murray, 1904).

---, *'The Irish Dramatic Movement'* in *Plays And Controversies* (London: Macmillan, 1923).

[1] Seamus Heaney, *Electric Light* (London, 2001), 46.

[2] W.B. Yeats, Preface to Augusta Gregory, *Gods and Fighting Men*, 14.

[3] Kieran Egan, *Teaching as Storytelling*.

[4] Peter Abbs, *A is for aesthetic: essays on creative and aesthetic education* (New York and London, 1989), 172.

[5] Seamus Heaney, *Wintering Out* (London,1972), 64.

[6] Yeats, Preface to *Gods and Fighting Men* , 14.

[7] W.B. Yeats, 'The Irish Dramatic Movement' in *Plays and Controversies*, 9.

[8] Yeats, *Plays and Controversies*, 9.

[9] Augusts Gregory, *Our Irish Theatre*, 213.

[10] Yeats, Preface to *Gods and Fighting Men,* 12.

[11] Gregory, *Our Irish Theatre*, 255.

[12] See S. Banaji, A.Burn and Buckingham, *The Rhetorics of Creativity: a review of the literature*.

[13] Jerome Bruner, *Actual Minds, Possible Worlds*, 126.

4 | Mirror, dynamo or lens?:
Drama, children, and social change
Jonothan Neelands

This essay builds on a series of bullet points which I prepared as the basis for my contribution to the Seamus Heaney Lecture Series. I have never been comfortable with the idea of speech where this means reading out a 'finished' lecture. For me, this oral recitation of a given and closed text short-circuits the essential 'liveness' of a shared public event. It asks an audience to listen to what they could read for themselves and at their leisure in some other context. It is an important feature of my own work as a drama practitioner that when people come together for the purpose of making theatre there should be some room for improvisation and dialogue, for responding to the here and now, for serendipitous happenings that could not have been planned for in advance or even repeated again. For this reason I wanted to give a 'talk' rather than a lecture.

As it was, the 'unexpected' drama of the event nearly unseated me and threatened to leave me without even the small props I had prepared in order to build my talk in action. I stood at the lectern and realized with horror that the notes I had so carefully placed earlier were missing! I asked again and again where my notes were. The audience laughed imagining that this was some playful ruse. This call and no response went on for some minutes and I was in total panic now. And then a soft voice came from the audience: 'Oh, I think I might have taken your notes.' It was Mr. Seamus Heaney himself who had just introduced the lecture without the need for any notes, but in leaving the lectern had, perhaps by force of habit, collected all the papers including my own and returned to his seat.

So this is the remains of the speech that Seamus Heaney stole from me!

In this talk I will outline a collection of metaphors in search of an idea that can express theatre's potential as a form of social pedagogy and socialization both for young people of school age and also for its other audiences and makers. In talking of a pedagogy of theatre I will borrow from the late John McGrath's use of the term a 'learning paedia' which he succinctly distils into two main features:

> Accuracy – the audience must recognize and accept the emotional and social veracity of what is happening on stage, must identify with the core situation, whatever style may be used to present it.

> Relevance – the core situation must reflect the central, most profound realities of its time, must speak to its audiences about a truth that matters in their lives, whether social, moral, political, emotional or individual I [1]

To these features of truthfulness and relevance he adds the core principle that theatre should use all possible means to reach every citizen and not act as 'an excluding agency, whether by the price of its tickets, the manner of its box office staff, its location or its impenetrability' (ibid., p.139).

To this idea of an inclusive 'paedia' in theatre I want to add at the outset a further pre-condition for a pro-social theatre which is captured most fully by the idea of 'ensemble' which is given fuller treatment at the close of this discussion on metaphors. For now, Mikhail Stronin, dramaturg of the Maly St Petersburg Theatre, provides us with a succinct description of the ensemble as 'one body with many heads, but many heads working in the same direction'. This desire to create pro-social theatre through collaboration, co-artistry and sophisticated uses of social intelligence forms the matrix for the discussion of metaphors.

Theatre as mirror; using God's scissors

This search for a meaningful metaphor for a pedagogic theatre is of course prompted by the use of the most well known – Mirror up to Nature – as title for this lecture series which is also subtitled as Drama in the Modern World. The metaphor of theatre as mirror offers a particular take on the ideas of accuracy and relevance, which is that theatre 'merely' reflects ourselves to ourselves. There is a suggestion that the life likeness of a mirrored reflection is a guarantee of its accuracy, authenticity and 'naturalness'.

> Speak the speech, I pray you as I pronounced it to you –
> trippingly on the tongue ... Suit the action to the word, the word
> to the action, with this special observation: that you o'erstep
> not the modesty of nature. For anything so overdone is from
> the purpose of playing, whose end, both at the first and now,
> was and is to hold as 'twere the mirror up to nature, to show
> virtue her own feature, scorn her own age, and the very body of
> the time his form and pressure (Hamlet 111,ii. 1-45).

What Hamlet asks of the players is to tell his story as if it was the only story in town. It is a monologic, representative and authored account of the 'truth' of his father's death. He demands that the players adopt what would become known as a 'naturalistic' style of performance without any exaggerated or 'unreal' gestures. In Hamlet's mind the 'truth' of events will be confirmed by the 'realism' of the playing. The more life-like the actions, the more convincing the argument of his story. Hamlet imagines that by stripping away all that is artificial in the players' performance they will appear to be more authentic; more true to life. And this criterion of authenticity and 'life-likeness' is still key to our aesthetic judgments of theatre.

In encouraging his actors, Hamlet makes a qualitative distinction between a 'realistic' performance for the educated courtiers and the 'dumb shows and noise' associated with the 'unskillful' and the 'groundlings'. We have here the beginnings of a tradition of a serious literary theatre, exclusive to certain classes, which distances itself both from the profane tastes and preferences of the lower orders and also from their world view. To the idea that theatrical naturalism is closer to the truth than other forms of representation is now added the political idea that the 'mirror' belongs to an educated elite with the sensibility to discern the 'accuracy' and 'relevance' in a performance of scientific verisimilitude.

The play within a play here is no mere entertainment. It is not planned as an evening's escape from the cares of office for Claudius and Gertrude – it is intended to be effective as a means of exposing their betrayal of the murdered king and so to directly bring about their downfall. So, Hamlet introduces another theme associated with the 'educated' theatre which is that it can illuminate and reveal the world and bring about a result or change in those who attend it.

This speech, with its iconic metaphor of the 'mirror unto nature', is often seen as presaging what has become the dominant genre of theatrical and dramatic representation in the West. The tradition of 'realism', which has its origins in a specific interpretation of Aristotle's concept of 'mimesis' and the close relationship between politics, philosophy and tragedy in 5th Century Athens, conflates reality with realism and realism as a style with truth. It is based in a belief that external appearances can mirror the soul. That only that which can be directly apprehended through the senses, exists. There is no room in this educated sensibility for a theatre of dream worlds, ghosts, demons and other spirits. This positivist and pragmatic world view bridges the Early Modernism of Shakespeare's age with the scientific rationalism and fatalism that would shape the Modernist aesthetics and theatres of the 19th and early 20th centuries with their obsessions with forensic accuracies of setting and acting.

The Western tradition of 'realism' underpins both the canonical 'serious' theatre associated with the subsidized sector and also the daily entertainments offered on TV and film. In the case of the subsidized theatre, this realism is associated with a literary tradition of authored plays offering an authoritative and authorized interpretation of an individual world view. Just as Hamlet authors the play within a play in his own likeness. In both cases the conflation of realism with reality serves to naturalize the specifically cultural and self-interested 'imaginaries' of certain social and cultural groups. The tradition of a subsidized theatre serving the interests of a few goes back to the Athenian tragedies which as Arnold Hauser (1999) and Augusto Boal (1998) argue were little more than apologies and propaganda for aristocratic rule. The tragedies tell the stories of princes and kings not slaves and women. The gods are to be served. The more popular but crude and distinctly un-realistic mimes and satyr plays of Athens required no subsidy; they were popular enough with the masses to be afforded. And Hamlet is of course speaking as an aristocrat planning a performance for his own class. He seeks to naturalize his own aristocratic world view and to present his perspective of the world as the only legitimate one. As if it was scientifically proven.

In popular forms of realism, the naturalizing of specifically cultural and social perspectives can feed any number of phobic injustices from racism to misogyny and homophobia. To what extent are Ballykissangel or Father Ted true mirrors of the nature of the

Irish, for instance? Both sacred and profane forms of drama contain the same trick which is to reassure ourselves that the order of things is as we imagine it. In both forms we continuously naturalize the politics and world view of a powerful few.

The cultural power of the 'mirror' and the naturalistic fallacy it contains – that behavioural realism is more accurate and truthful than other styles of theatre representation – spreads into the education domain as well. Drama in Education for instance, also holds to the idea that by 'living through' human experiences in a 'realistic' and 'life like' way in real time young people will discover the 'truth' of human existences which they can only imagine and never in reality know. Living through the experiences of peoples who are temporally, spatially, culturally, and socio-economically different 'as if' these experience were actually happening here and now for the participants in a Process Drama, is seen as being more truthful and 'life like' a learning experience than other more stylized and self-reflexive forms of theatre. In truth, whatever the appearance may be, we can only ever learn more about our own personal and collective self through imagining ourselves differently. We may develop empathy and understanding from our experiences of 'playing' others but we cannot in actuality walk in shoes other than our own. Spending four hours or more in the classroom 'building investment' and 'belief' in an imagined character and situation prior to an 'authentic' role play is in fact a mythologized dilution of the working practices of Stanislavski, Michael Chekhov and their followers who constitute the historical and contemporary face of behavioural realism in acting.

But at least Hamlet seeks a form of theatrical representation that has social agency. This is the idea that the world is changeable, not determined, and that through the agency of theatre we may come to understand the power of human action in shaping destiny. As Raymond Williams (1954) commented, whilst the genre of action drama would become increasingly the domain of commercial film, the trajectory in serious theatre since Shakespeare, has been towards a theatre of social inaction and passivity. A theatre which suggests that there is nothing that can be done. That human agency is impotent in the face of a world claimed and owned by the powerful whether they be aristocrats or the educated middle classes. That the world if not determined is at least determining of human existence. This tendency towards the passive inaction of social and artistic actors, already suggested by Hamlet's inability to act to right the wrongs done to his father, finds its *apogée* in *Waiting for Godot* where nothing at all happens –ever !

If there is nothing that can be shown to be done, the Mirror becomes a place for narcissistic gazes into the individual rather than the social psyche. A theatre of introspection, fixity and stasis rather than of action. A psychological theatre of the individual trapped in an unchangeable world, suffering an inevitable destiny beyond self control. The social self of collective public action in the agora that characterized the early Athenian polis, of renaissance England, of the other great social and revolutionary movements of the 19th century becomes in the mid/late 20th century the privatized and psychologized self haunting empty and closed rooms, literally blinded, and searching for the truth within rather than seeking it without. Until Sarah Kane so exquisitely collides the intimate with the public, the epically tragic with the banally domestic in *Blasted*, in which the unavoidable ugliness of the world beyond crashes at last through the fourth wall of self-protecting and privileged illusion.

In any case the origins of the 'naturalistic' theatre lie in the origins of a representative democracy in Athens. It is not the theatre of a direct or participatory democracy. Hamlet does not design a theatrical meeting between his story and Claudius's or his mother's or any of the other multiple voices entangled in his plot. He speaks for all. Just as in our own politics, we still rely on theatre in our 'representatives' to tell the theatrical truth and make our decisions for us. We are shown the world 'as it is' rather than forging the world as we see it could be from our diverse perspectives. The technical term for the 'realist' style of acting which would become codified as a method by Stanislavski and his followers is 'representational'. Actors create a world for a distant audience as if the fictive world exists independently from the actual world of the spectator. There is no communication or communion between actors and audiences. There is no dialogue; it is monologic and monolithic. There is no interaction of ideas or posing of alternatives. The alternative mode of performance, which is closely associated with Bertolt Brecht is named 'presentational' and does make direct contact between performers and audience and may well include interaction and banter. There is a direct correspondence between the fictive world of the stage and the actual world of the audience. This tradition belongs to the history of popular forms of entertainment and despite Hamlet's disparagements is often cited as an example of Shakespeare's plays being popular with the 'groundlings' who were seldom quiet in their gaze on the 'mirror' of theatre. It is part of my argument here that the theatre of direct democracy must be a participatory theatre which is made by all who engage with it. A theatre in which the roles of social and artistic actor are fluid and transposable. A theatre which negotiates different perspectives of the world and different possibilities for changing it. A theatre which is more like a hologram or a kaleidoscope than a finely focussed and well lit mirror.

In a recent survey final year English students at my own University were asked whether they preferred an active approach to their core Shakespeare course rather than lectures and seminars. 87% of respondents preferred lectures to a more active exploration of the plays as actors. Of these 67% disclosed a fear and in some cases 'hatred' of acting. In a theatre of mirrors we cease to see ourselves as actors in either the social and artistic spheres. Both require public action in a public engagement and for these students at least this idea of public action, acting up to make things happen, is terrifying.

And of course we also need to trouble the metaphor of the mirror even further. Whose mirror is it? Who holds it up and what is their relationship to the viewer/subject? Is it a kind mirror? Does it flatter or demean the viewer? Does it tell the truth – whose truth? Does it dare to 'o'erstep the modesty of nature? Does it offer a mirror of reality or a comfortable escape in which 'temperance may give it smoothness'? These were not innocent questions for Shakespeare and the King's Men, writing and performing during a period of emergent republicanism in England. The festivals of Athens, much like our own subsidized theatre, depended on producers and paymasters who were more likely to patronize work which confirmed their power and naturalized their influence within a 'democratic society'. There is always a Maecenas – the one who pays the piper.

These questions around the ownership of the means and processes of theatrical representation and whose world view is naturalized are of course critical for our young people. We live now in a world of mirrors seemingly held up to nature. Much of what young people know about the world beyond their own immediate experience is through the representations of the mass media and the prejudices of their own communities. They need to be helped towards a more critical and challenging response to the truth of the Murdoch News and other mediated pictures of the world beyond.

In his poem, 'On Leaving the Theatre', Edward Bond (1978) captures these questions in the following words:

> To make the play the writer used god's scissors
> Whose was the pattern?
> The actors rehearsed with care
> Have they moulded you to their shape?
> Has the lighting man blinded you?
> The designer dressed your ego?
> You cannot live on our wax fruit
> Leave the theatre hungry
> For change.[2]

What I have described here is the politics of the 'naturalistic fallacy' in theatre; the politics behind the idea that the more realistic a piece of theatre is the more truthful it is. Despite Hamlet's tutoring the play that follows will of course be artificial – it cannot be real in the sense that daily living is real, because it is a conscious and selective human reworking of reality. It is necessarily false to nature in this sense, however life-like it might appear to be. It is 'artifice' rather than 'reality' that gives theatre its power. Theatre gives human shape and form to experience in order to hold it for a while as if it was reflected in a mirror but as an abominable imitation of humanity not as lived experience itself. This power is contained in the gap between how we experience the world and how it is mirrored to us. In the differences as much as in the similarities. The truth is neither in our own subjective experience nor in the play – it emerges through the dialectic and dialogue between.

> Theatre as dynamo; man is a helper to man
> I am a playwright. I show
> What I have seen. At the markets of men
> I have seen how men are bought and sold. This
> I, the playwright, show.
> How they step into each other's room with plans
> Or with rubber truncheons or with money
> How they stand and wait on the streets
> How they prepare snares for each other
> Full of hope
> How they make appointments
> How they string each other up
> How they love each other
> How they defend the spoils

How they eat
That is what I show ... (from: 'The Playwright's Song' by Bertolt
Brecht)

This second metaphor is borrowed from Darko Suvin's paper on
Brecht's aesthetics titled The Mirror and the Dynamo (1968). Suvin
argues that the mirror metaphor is more appropriately applied to
what he calls the aesthetics of 'illusionism – taking for granted that
an artistic representation in some mystic ways reproduces or 'gives'
man and the world'. In its place he offers a new scientific metaphor
for Brecht's theatre with its origins in the idea of the promethean
human potential to create and use transformative energy and action
to better the world. In Brecht's take on Modernism, there is the
belief that theatre and the arts can be catalytic to the wider human
struggle to determine the world rather than be determined by it.
Brecht assumes this action will be associated with the creation of
egalitarian democracies to replace the aristocratic and totalitarian
systems of governance which dominated his age and place. Indeed
Brecht referred to his work as symbolic action rather than as
representation. Suvin explains the metaphor thus:

> Art is not a mirror which reflects the truth existing outside the
> artist: art is not a static representation of a given Nature in
> order to gain the audience's empathy: Brecht sees art as a
> dynamo, an artistic and scenic vision which penetrates Nature's
> possibilities, which finds out the 'co-variant' laws of its
> processes and makes it possible for critical understanding to
> intervene into them.[3]

Brecht's idea of truthfulness is quite different from that of the
search for 'authentic' appearances that characterizes the theatre of
mirrors. Brecht seeks illumination rather than illusion. To show how
things work, to whom they belong, whose interests are served and
how this might be changed. Brecht's aim was to reveal the world, to
look behind the mirror, to ask questions of it, not merely to reflect a
particular and naturalized illusion of it. It is a reflection on nature,
not of nature. Suvin argues that Brecht's dramaturgy presupposed
that the audience were seeing the work from the perspective of a
utopian future 'an imaginary just and friendly future, where man is a
helper to man'.

Brecht reclaims a theatre of action that is more concerned with
the sociology of human behaviour and the dynamics of history than
with the inner psychological workings of alienated individuals. One

of his models was Shakespeare's Histories with their emphasis on human action and the forging of futures through human agency rather than through fate or destiny. He was drawn to the epic scale of the Histories which moved rapidly from place to place without the fussiness of 'naturalistic' sets and to the idea that seventy or more years of history could be distilled into three hours of playing.

In terms of the aesthetics of the theatre as dynamo, it is well known that Brecht insisted that the means of production were made as visible as possible to the audience and that the work was inclusive of a wide range of performance traditions associated both with the popular theatre and other entertainments associated with the working classes and also from other great 'non-realist' performance traditions including the Chinese Opera.

> We shall make lively use of all means, old and new, tried and untried, deriving from art and deriving from other sources, in order to put living reality in the hands of living people in such a way that it can be mastered.[4]

Rather than creating an illusion for an audience of 'peeping toms' (as Artaud (1938) once described the naturalistic theatre's patrons), Brecht kept reminding his audience that they were engaging with an 'artifice' a conscious and transparent construction of the world according to his own Marxist principles. He showed that we can bring the world closer by moving it further away – by de-familiarizing it and making it strange so that it has to be consciously and cognitively re-recognized by a critical and conscious audience hungry for change. Brecht turned events on their head shattering the comfortable illusion of cause and effect which characterizes the 'realist' narrative. Making his audience think about the story rather than merely hear it. If accuracy of 'realistic' detail marks the metaphor of the mirror, it is the accuracy and cognitive adequacy of the account of human history which characterizes the metaphor of the dynamo. Brecht's actors were still 'representatives' but they combined the social within the artistic in their acting – the stage actor as social actor acting the part of a social actor on stage. In Brecht's world we are all social actors making our destiny as living people.

If one puts aside for a moment Brecht's unwavering faith in the scientific 'truth' of Marxism and allow for a less certain but still critical attitude both to theatre making and to the changeable world theatre represents, there are some attractions in the metaphor of the dynamo when we consider what kind of theatre young people deserve.

There is for me a welcome honesty in the dynamo metaphor – there is no attempt to create a seductive and partial 'mirror' of the world. There is the hope, at least, that through our own individual and collective social acting we can change the world and ourselves. There is a commitment to justice and to social responsibility and to a theatre that shows us how and why the world is often an unfair place. In its gaze from the synoptic vantage point of a utopian future it promises a glimpse of justice and authentic democracy to the young who are becoming the future. It is a theatre which demonstrates both through its treatment of the world and through its means of production that the social, educational and political structures we work within are capable of being re-imagined and transformed by creative human action. The Canadian literary theorist Northrop Frye (1963) wrote that: 'The fundamental job of the imagination in ordinary life, then, is to produce, out of the society we have to live in, a vision of the society we want to live in'.

There is here a belief in our individual and collective capacity to act in and on the world in ways that are original and significant. This belief that we are individually and collectively able to re-make ourselves, our technologies, our cultures and common life offers young people a doctrine of hope in the hard times ahead.

At the heart of a pro-social, action-based dynamo metaphor of theatre is the vibrant tension between structure (constraints) and agency (freedom to act). Being creative means acting to shape the structures that shape us; controlling and shaping nature as well as cultural institutions. Prometheus stole fire from the gods artfully, and with that fire man created warmth, shelter, technology and culture. The primal shaping structure is nature, and throughout history mankind has shown that through human action, nature can be overcome and transformed rather than merely mirrored or copied.

Theatre as lens; acting to learn, learning to act

I want to now add a third metaphor of my own crafting which is that of theatre as a lens – as a window for looking into 'nature', rather than as a surface that reflects it or copies it. This metaphor has its origins in a book I wrote in the 80s as a young teacher about my own first experiences in using drama in the classroom (Neelands 1984). I wanted to try and capture the relationship between drama, the curriculum and the teacher and learners. I suggested that in a conventional transmission model, what is being learnt about is only really seen by the teacher. The teacher stands between the learners and what they are learning about and decides what they should know and when and how it should be interpreted. This model is described by Basil Bernstein (1973) as a 'collection code', a rigid and insulated subject-based curriculum which isolates the 'legitimized' knowledge to be acquired in the classroom from the everyday knowledges beyond the school and which is supported by the authority of the teacher as the one who knows. Bernstein described the effects thus:

> Knowledge under collection is private property with its own power structure and market situation ... children and pupils are early socialized into this concept of knowledge as private property. They are encouraged to work as isolated individuals with their arms around their work.[5]

and

> The frames of the collection code, very early in the child's life, socialize him into knowledge frames which discourage connections with everyday realities.[6]

Here is an example which captures the difference between a theatre-as-lens approach to learning and a normative curriculum approach. A class of urban eight-year-olds in role as 'landscape gardeners' are asked by the teacher in role as the Head Teacher of a Special School, to create a garden for her pupils some of whom are visually impaired and some of whom use wheelchairs. The pupils are asked to use their 'expert' knowledge to design a suitable landscape for the garden and suggest appropriate planting so that all of the pupils can get enjoyment and access the garden. The Head Teacher also wants her pupils to be involved in looking after the garden.

In order for the landscape gardeners to present their plan to the Head Teacher, they must research the needs of visually impaired and wheelchair bound children; which flowers and plants might offer textures and smells for visually impaired people; how to design the garden so that it is interesting and accessible for wheelchair users; how sounds and textures might be used; how to design and build paths and beds so that wheelchair users can do some gardening themselves.

In addition to this work, pupils will also have to consider the maths of the project – how big the space is, how big beds and other features will be, how many plants will be needed etc. They may also look in science at why plants have scents and which insects, like butterflies, might be attracted by certain plants. From a technology perspective they might also consider how to install a watering system on a timer so that the garden users don't have to struggle with hosepipes and watering cans, or they might invent their own self-watering system using collected rain water.

In fact the lens offered here is 'imagined experience' rather than an optical object or tool; learning through being in a dramatized situation and a role that requires researched and responsible action. Learning through imagined experience allows us to engage with learning, directly, physically, contextually, with real life purposes and motives. Theatre in all its forms has this capacity to engage our emotions very directly in the lives of others and in situations which are beyond our own daily experience. To feel for them and want to do something positive. Freud reminds is that 'Art is a conventionally accepted reality in which, thanks to artistic illusion, symbols and substitutes are able to provoke real emotions.'[7]

This enactive and inquiry based model of learning fits well with Margaret Donaldson's argument in a chapter with the beautiful title of *The Shape of Minds to Come*:

> By the time they come to school, all normal children can show skill as thinkers and language users, which must compel our respect, so long as they are dealing with 'real-life' meaningful situations in which they can recognize and respond to similar purposes and intentions in others. These human intentions are the matrix in which the child's thinking is embedded. They sustain and direct his thought and speech, just as they sustain and direct the thought and speech of adults – even intellectually sophisticated adults – most of the time.

The lens metaphor of theatre is commonly associated with those forms of improvised and participatory drama which make up the 'Process Drama' tradition in schools. One of its leading exponents, John O'Toole and his co-author Julie Dunn describe it in these words:

> In the classroom there is no outside audience. Most of the time we are improvising with the children, exploiting fictional situations through various kinds of role-play, mixed with

theatrical and dramatic conventions, games and exercises. We
call this working in 'Process Drama', which is like children's
play, with all the players actively involved.[8]

This process approach to theatre making presupposes a radical
shift in the relationship between theatre and its audiences. In the
popular imagination, theatre is often thought of as the performance
of plays by professional or amateur actors to a paying audience. It is
a picture of theatre that is based on an economic agreement between
the producers and the audience. The producers rehearse and
develop a theatre product to the best of their abilities and when the
time comes, they perform their work in exchange for the price of a
ticket.

More often than not, in Western forms of theatre, the product
that is exchanged is based on the work of a playwright. There is an
assumption in this model of theatre that the majority of us will see
rather than be in such plays. Acting, producing theatre, is seen as
something only a few can achieve. There is also the assumption that
the audience in this literary theatre will be silent and attentive to the
work of the actors – audience responses are private rather than
publicly shared as they might be in more popular forms of
entertainment.

If this popular image of theatre is the dominant one in most
Western societies it should be remembered that there are alternative
models of community theatre and performance which may bring us
closer to recognizing drama-making in schools as theatre.

In local communities in my society and in many traditional
societies, the arts still serve the important civic and community
functions that ritual and art-making once provided for us all. In the
so-called golden ages of Athenian and Elizabethan drama, going to
the theatre was an important and integral part of the public life of
the citizen. The theatre still offers communities a public forum for
debating, affirming and challenging culture and community ties. In
this community model, the arts are seen as important 'means' of
representing and commenting on the cultural life and beliefs of the
community, in turn the communal participation of the whole
community in art-making strengthens their cultural bonds. Every
member of the group is seen as a potential producer – a potential
artist. In this model, theatre is produced on the basis of a social
agreement between members of a group who come together to make
something that will be of importance to them; something that will
signify their lives.

This alternative social and community model of theatre shares some of the characteristics of drama in schools. A school is a community and drama is a living practice within it. The drama that young people make is often based in the concerns, needs and aspirations shared within the school community, or the community of a particular teaching group. It is often based on a social agreement that all who are present are potential producers – everyone can have a go at being actors and/or audience as the drama progresses. The coming together to make drama is also often seen as an important means of making the teaching group more conscious of themselves as a living community.

Theatre can offer young people a mirror of who we are and who we are becoming. Theatre can be a dynamo for social change by providing the space to imagine ourselves and how we live differently. Theatre can be a lens through which young people can discover the embodied relevance of the real in the curriculum. But beyond these optic metaphors is the most important – the social metaphor of the ensemble as a model for living together in the world. Through acting together in the making of ensemble-based theatre, young people are provided with what Trevor Nunn calls 'an ideal of a world I want to live in'. The ensemble provides the basis for young people to develop the complex levels of social intelligence (Gardner 1988) needed to embrace the challenges of the future, whilst also developing the social imagination required to produce collaborative social art which reflects, energizes and focuses the world for young people. The social knowing which comes from acting in an ensemble mirrors Friere's concept of 'indispensable' knowledge:

> The kind of knowledge that becomes solidarity, becomes a 'being with'. In that context, the future is seen, not as inexorable, but as something that is constructed by people engaged together in life, in history. It's the knowledge that sees history as possibility and not as already determined – the world is not finished. It is always in the process of becoming.[9]

Working together in the social and egalitarian conditions of the ensemble, young people have the opportunity to struggle with the demands of become a self-managing, self-governing, self-regulating social group who co-create artistically and socially. It is better to be in an ensemble than a gang. The ensemble is a bridging metaphor between the social and the artistic; between the informal uses of classroom drama and professional theatre. Michael Boyd, Artistic Director of the RSC, captures this duality in his support for ensemble based theatre:

> We've never had more cause to realize the grave importance of our interdependence as humans and yet we seem ever more incapable of acting on that realization with the same urgency that we all still give to the pursuit of self interest. Theatre does have a very important role because it is such a quintessentially collaborative art form.

The principles of the ensemble require the uncrowning of the power of the director/teacher, a mutual respect amongst the players, a shared commitment to truth, a sense of the intrinsic value of theatre making, a shared absorption in the artistic process of dialogic and social meaning making. The social experience of acting as an ensemble, making theatre that reflects and suggests how the world might become, in the hope that it is not finished, is of course of paramount importance to our young. We pass them the burden of the world that we have made in the hope that they will in turn have a world to pass on to their children. In this task socially made theatre will be their mirror, dynamo and lens – their tool for change.

Bibliography

Artaud, A., *Theatre and its Double*, trans. Mary Caroline Richards (New York: Grove Press, 1958).

Bernstein, B., *Class, Codes and Control*, vol 1 (St. Albans: Paladin, 1973).

Boal, A., *Theatre of the Oppressed* (London: Pluto Press, 1998).

Bond, E., *Theatre Poems and Songs* (London: Eyre: Methuen, 1978).

Brecht, B. 'The Popular and the Realistic'. *Twentieth Century Theatre: A Sourcebook*, ed. Richard Drain (London and New York: Routledge, 1995), 188-91.

Freire, P., *Pedagogy of Freedom* (Oxford: Rowmann and Littlefield, (1998).

Hauser, A. *The Social History of Art - from prehistoric times to the middle ages* vol. 1 (London and New York: Routledge, 1999).

Longman Suvin, D. (1967) 'The Mirror and the Dynamo; on Brecht's aesthetic point of view', *TDR* Vol 12 No 1 pages 56-67.

McGrath, J. 'Theatre and Democracy', *New Theatre Quarterly* no. 18 May 2002.

Neelands, J. *Making Sense of Drama* (London; Heinemann, 1984).

O'Toole, J. and J. Dunn, *Pretending to Learn* (Frenchs Forest, NSW: (2002).

Petocz, A. *Freud, Psychoanalysis and Symbolism* (Cambridge: CUP, 1999).

Williams, R. *Drama in Performance* (Harmondsworth: Penguin, 1954).

---

[1] John McGrath, 'Theatre and Democracy', *New Theatre Quarterly,* 18 May 2002.

[2] Edward Bond, 'On Leaving the Theatre' from *Theatre Poems and Songs* (London, 1978), 5.

[3] D. Suvin, 'The Mirror and the Dynamo; on Brecht's Aesthetic Point of View", *TDR* 12, 1, 56-57.

[4] Bertolt Brecht, *'The Popular and the Realistic', American Theatre : a Sourcebook*, ed. Richard Drain (London and New York. 1995), 188-91.

[5] Basil Bernstein, *Class, Codes and Control* (St Albans, 1973), 240.

[6] Ibid., 242.

[7] Cf. A. Petocz, *Freud, Psychoanalysis and Symbolism*, 93.

[8] J.O' Toole and J. Dunn, *Pretending to Learn.*

[9] P. Freire, *Pedagogy of Freedom*, 72.

5 | From Boucicault to Beckett: From Real to Reel (1894-20)

Brenna Katz Clarke

This article began life as a lecture for the Seamus Heaney Series, 'The Mirror Up to Nature'. (March 2007, St Patrick's College, Drumcondra) Footage from films ranging from the Lumière Brothers to *Singin' in the Rain* was used to illustrate aspects of a visual medium. Where a film clip was shown, the film will be mentioned so that the reader might refer back to these films, but inevitably something is lost in this format.

The relationship between film and theatre has been the subject of film and literary discourse since film began its short history, just over a hundred years ago. The dynamics of difference between theatre and film is a vast subject, despite cinema's short story compared to the long history of theatre. Some of these differences and points of convergence will be part of my discourse. As 'Holding the Mirror Up to Nature' was the overriding theme of the Seamus Heaney Lecture series, this dynamic will be considered among others. Due to the enormous breadth of the subject, topics are merely a montage of impressions to tempt the reader to think and read further.

Dr Bernard Beckerman's seminal book *The Dynamics of Drama* (1970) devised a method of analysis for theatre, which still stands as a useful Poetics for today. In his book, he stresses performance over literature and presents a useful definition of theatre: 'Theater occurs when one or more human beings isolated in time and space, present themselves to another or others'. Had he lived, Beckerman would have undoubtedly had much to say about film, especially Shakespeare on film. In homage to Beckerman's work, this article will use the notion of Dynamics to explore the variety of differences and similarities between theatre and film.

The Russian symbolist poet Alexander Blok (1880-1921) wrote to a friend:

> In my opinion cinema has nothing in common with theatre, is not attached to it, does not compete with it, nor can they destroy each other ... Film found a new technique for itself ... and far from destroying each other, film and theatre have continued to evolve and develop each in its own way, sometimes diverging, sometimes converging, but always exercising a powerful and mutual influence upon each other.[1]

The Dynamic of Danger and Destruction

Peter Brook in his seminal work *The Empty Space* wrote: 'We talk of the cinema killing the theatre.'[2] The language used by Brook paints cinema, the upstart who is only 113 years old, as somehow dangerous. A certain fear of film has existed from its earliest inception. The cinema has at times been considered a threat to theatre, even as television has been cited as the killer of both film and theatre. Film and later television have also been named as threats to literature and to the act of reading books.

Educators feared that film would steal children away from reading. Although it has been said that more young people are now cineaste than literate, the reality is that cinema has brought many back to reading and back into the theatre.

As part of the process of adaptation, many children and adults are brought back to a book, having seen 'the film.' Children who have loved the Harry Potter films are tempted to read the books. The recent successful Wicked (the back-story musical of Wizard of Oz) attracted dozens of children to the theatre. The box office sold copies of the original book *The Wonderful Wizard of Oz* (by L. Frank Baum, 1900) alongside the obligatory t-shirts and CDs and children were buying them, creating new readers of the classic.

Film seems also to have usurped the dodgy reputation that theatre once held with Noel Coward's warning: 'Don't put your daughter on the stage, Mrs Worthington.' Hollywood has acquired associations of glamour, sex, gossip and Scientology. In the course of his words of acceptance for the 2009 Academy Award for Best Actor (in *Milk*), Sean Penn addressed the audience as 'you commie homo loving sons of guns', playing on the liberal tradition of the Academy and the film world.

Yet film has gained respectability: it now appears on the Irish Leaving Certificate examination and on the syllabus of even the most canonical English Department courses. Whereas for many, theatre is considered staid, traditional and safe – and a medium for the elite!

Theatre and cinema have fed each other, competed with each other, embraced each other, and been intertwined from film's beginnings. Actors, directors and writers have always moved freely between the stage and cinema and more recently television.

Helen Mirren who won the best-actress Oscar for the film *The Queen* (2007) was quoted:

> Most of the cast of *The Queen* have spent most of their careers on the stage. My own career has included productions with companies like the Royal Shakespeare Company and the National Theatre, and I'm sure it won't be long before I'm back on the stage. (*Guardian*, 16 Feb. 2007).

Actors like Kevin Spacey move freely between acting in plays, films and his role as Artistic Director of the Old Vic Company in London. Everyone, from film actors Nicole Kidman to Sienna Miller, has done a stint in the theatre. Even D.W. Griffith, the great actor, director and playwright, started his career in a temporary acting job, under the name Lawrence Griffith. He got a small bit part, which started his career at the Edison Studios in the Bronx in 1907.

This intermingling highlights the fact that affinities between the two forms are more interesting than their differences, though more critical attention has been devoted to the latter. Theatre can sometimes be described as cinematic. Likewise cinema, from blockbusters to the work of the auteurs, can be regarded as highly theatrical.

James Hurt, Professor Emeritus at the University of Illinois, in his important book, *Focus on Film and Theatre*, 1974, highlights the points of similarity between the two forms that both tell stories:

> Both are performance arts that ordinarily involve an audience gathering at a prescribed time in a theatre to witness a scheduled event (like dance and live music and unlike painting, sculpture and novels).[3]

Rudolf Arnheim in his 1933 *Film as Art* writes:

> There are still many-educated people who stoutly deny the possibility that film might be art. They say, in effect: ' Film

cannot be art, for it does not but reproduce reality mechanically
...Can one justify our denying photography and film a place in
the temple of the Muses?[4]

The Dynamic of History – The Beginnings

The history of the theatre is that of an ancient art, one going back
beyond the fifth century BC and the golden age of Greek Theatre. It
began in the early fertility rites of the ancient Greeks and the singing
of dithyrambs to the god Dionysus and was closely related to fertility
and to religion. It was a primal theatre of myth, story telling, choral
activity and ecstasy. Patrick Mason evoked the spirit of Dionysus in
his brilliant opening lecture and Dionysus presided over the entire
Heaney series.

Cinema on the other hand has a baby history, 115 years,
depending on when you date the beginning. The god of cinema is
more connected to the little statue, Oscar, and the god of money.
Religion is often confined to the epics of Charlton Heston's *Ben Hur*
or the films of Pasolini or Mel Gibson.

The early history of cinema has been more a history of
technology and inventions, gimmickry and commerce. The story has
been less important than the 'pitch.' The studio system, the star
system, the commercialism and the glamorous world of escapism
have all been linked to the history of cinema.

What then is the different dynamic in history of theatre and
cinema – one born out of myth, religion and fertility rites, the other
born from science and photography? Both were, at the beginning,
popular forms of entertainment. Only later do we see a divide
between the public and the private forms of theatre and indeed the
popular and the elite in cinema.

The actress Cate Blanchett in an interview was asked whether she
might be interested in directing a film:

> I don't know if I'm interested in film. It's a very technical
> medium and I'm a complete Luddite. I instinctively understand
> space as an actor – the shifts of the chess pieces around a board
> – but I don't know that I have the natural objectivity you need
> for film. (*Guardian* 13/1/07)

The early history of film was indeed very technical. In the early
period (1824-1832) inventors were interested in making images
move. Instead of the *deus ex machina* of the early Greek Theatre,
the early history of cinema is full of machines such as the

thaumatrope and the stroboscope, all creating animated pictures, the zoetrope mounting photographs on blades of a paddle wheel which was spun, the kinematoscope, the phasmatrope and Edison's Kinetograph.

The arrival of the Lumiere Brothers, August and Louis, in 1895, is often cited as the real birth of cinema. They invented and patented a projection machine in 1895, and began showing projected films for the first paying audience, often as part of vaudeville shows. Their work consisted mainly of realistic moving images taken from everyday life. The Lumiere Brothers created over 1,400 different short films, though Louis, the younger brother, we are told, declared that: 'The cinema is an invention without a future.'

The brothers thought people would get bored of images that they could just see in their everyday life. However, their film sequence of a train pulling into the station had audiences screaming and ducking for cover. They thought the train itself was about to hurtle into the theatre!

Georges Méliès (1861-1938) the French film maker began shooting and exhibiting films in 1896. He is seen as the pre-cursor of special effects and CGI in the cinema. His famous films such as *A Trip to the Moon*, 1902, pioneered some of the techniques that have come to characterize later filmmaking such as multiple exposures, time-lapse photographs, dissolves. Because of his ability to manipulate and transform reality, he was sometimes referred to as the Cinemagician. (Before making films he had been a real magician at the Theatre Robert-Houdini.) Méliès wanted to change reality with film, not simply to record it.

The Dynamic of Melodrama and Pictorial Realism

Melodrama has often been cited as the precursor of cinema. A. Nicholas Vardac, in his book *Stage to Screen, Theatrical origins of Early Film*, has charted the theatrical background to the growth of the cinema:

> The necessity for greater pictorial realism in the arts appears as the logical impetus to the invention of cinema. This aesthetic tension found its preliminary satisfaction in the theatrical forms preceding and surrounding the arrival of film.[5]

He examines the popular theatre's interest in pictorial theatre beginning with Garrick, through melodrama and the production styles of the Bancrofts, Henry Irving in England and David Belasco (1994-1930) and Steele MacKaye in America.

The plays, most of them as unmemorable as the well-made plays of Eugene Scribe, could have been written for silent pictures. They contain very little dialogue, depend on suspense and the development is presented visually through stage movement and sensation scenes. The audience saw real ships on real water that could sink, real locomotives colliding on stage, and realistic battle scenes before their amazed eyes.

Of the playwright-producers of the popular theatre of this period, none was more successful than Dion Boucicault. His highly popular work began mid-century and his contribution to cinema was considerable and significant. Some of his plays were made into the earliest feature films; his theatrical approach was highly cinematic.

Vardac and others argue that the development of film structure derives from this style of playwrighting and is the real beginning of cinematic syntax. In particular, Boucicault used what we now describe as filmic devices: fades, cross cutting, dissolves, tracking shots, escape scenes straight out of a disaster film.

Boucicault's popularity stemmed from his pictorial sensations. Boucicault's *The Poor of New York* (1857) was so popular that the same play was renamed *The Streets of London* or, *The Streets of Paris* etc. It is remembered for the scene of the burning tenement on stage where a real fire engine pulled by horses had to come on stage to put out the fire. Pictorial realism and sensationalism went hand in hand. According to W.S. Gilbert:

> Every play, which contains a house on fire, a sinking steamer, a railway accident, and a dance in a casino, will ... succeed in spite of itself. In point of fact, nothing could wreck such a piece but carefully written dialogue and strict attention to probability.[6]

The changes required to create these scenes were often unwieldy, given the conventional, old style staging with: wings, grooves, bridges, traps and flies, painted cloth drops lowered from the flies, where in a film, you would simply require a shift in the camera's position.

It was difficult for realism to prevail in this highly wrought presentational style of production. The nineteenth-century stage loved not only disasters, but weather with lots of snow, rain and sleet. Rain was managed in a number of ways. Audiences didn't need to see the rain, as the sound effect was created by the rain machine up in the flies, filled with dry peas, and real rain provided by a series of perforated pipes with a water supply. The real was often combined with the unreal. The problem was that the illusion was lost when there was rain because the actors remained dry as they acted in front of the scene.

Vardac claims such incongruity shows the final stage in the breakdown of the nineteenth-century staging methods. As realistic as this device might appear, it was still artificial. He claims that the motion picture was the natural heir to this entire pictorially minded theatre and only cinema could carry on the tradition. The earliest films adopted this popular realism and also stole away the popular audiences.

Of course, at the time that cinema was developing, the theatre itself was bifurcated. Alongside the commercial growth of vaudeville, light comedy melodrama, the birth of realism and naturalism was happening at the same time. Forgettable scripts of melodrama appeared at the same time as the works of Ibsen, Strindberg and Chekhov and the social drama of Shaw. In production values, realistic scenery had found the proscenium and the box scene with its fourth wall. So the newer and more realistic staging methods continued alongside those artificial conventions most regularly associated with melodrama. The late nineteenth century also saw the birth of new theatres and styles of acting,

Although acting in film and theatre is too large a topic to deal with in such a short article, the birth of Stanislavsky and his System in this period has direct implications for film acting, a method beloved of a whole school of actors from Brando to Pacino.

The Dynamic of Sound: The Sound Era

A real turning point in cinema came in late 1927 when Warner Brothers released *The Jazz Singer* with Al Jolson, directed by Alan Crosland, which was mostly silent, but had the first synchronized dialogue and singing in a feature film. It was a huge success and cinema changed forever. Many silent filmmakers and actors were not able to adjust and found their careers at an end. This is captured brilliantly in Stanley Donen's *Singin' in the Rain*.

The dynamic of sound and music is a vast topic. Soundscape is the term used for all sound in films. The technology has come a long way from silent films to Dolby surround, the Foley Effect and digitization. The director's use of a sound designer allows for the effects we have come to expect in film from non-diagetic sound tracks to diagetic footsteps, car crashes and the sounds of fighting. Psycho's famous shower scene creates violence through the orchestral sounds that simulate but do not show a killing. Menace is created through music in the film *Jaws*.

Theatre is full of sound but it is the effect of the non-verbal, the silent, that theatre perhaps does best. Beckett's and Pinter's use of dramatic and orchestrated silence is poetic and profound. Brecht's use of the silent scream when Mother Courage is shown the body of her dead son, Swiss Cheese, is more eloquent than the silence of the whirring camera.

Both film and theatre are visual, but the language of film speaks to us all in the way that music speaks to us. The closing image of the boy holding his father's hand in Vittorio De Sica's *Bicycle Thieves* needs no subtitles and needs no sound.

Joseph Conrad says that, in the novel, language gets in the way of what we really are trying to say and that that is the power of the cinema, yet Antonin Artaud describes the language of theatre as having the ability to express beyond the reach of the spoken language.[7]

The Dynamic of Structure

The basic unit of structure in a film is the shot, the basic unit in a play is the scene. A film shot is the smallest unit of cinematic language, the duration of a scene with no cuts. That film can be shot out of sequence is often cited as the most unique aspect of cinema.

In the theatre, we think of a play as composed of scenes and acts. Yet in Shakespeare's time, a unit of construction for the stage was the scene rather than the act. A play consisted of twenty or thirty scenes rather than three to five much longer acts.

(One could suggest that the cinematic nature of his plays is why there are more films of Shakespeare than any other playwright.)

By the nineteenth century, as theatre moved from the thrust stage to the proscenium arch and as realism became important, the longer, more realistic unit of the act became the norm.

August Strindberg in his important document on naturalism, the Preface to *Miss Julie*, calls for breaks in acts to be removed to create a greater illusion of reality. *Miss Julie* is structured as one long act with a mime in the middle to give the audience a breather. Strindberg stressed that in real life we don't have act breaks, or go out for a drink at intervals.

The Dynamic of Time

Time is the ultimate syntax of film. During the first decade of film making, the standard length of a film was about one reel or about ten to fifteen minutes long. The producers felt that the largely working class audience of the nickelodeons in the USA lacked attention span.

> One of the most liberating dynamics in the early development of film technique was that film need not be bound to the theatre's conventional use of continuous and sequential time.[8]

Editing allows an actor to jump locations in a way that is not possible in the theatre. The film has greater flexibility in merging time, presenting simultaneous action, going back and forth between past, present and future. The interesting thing is that we accept this as normal within the world of a film. Time-change in a film can be indicated by dissolves, wipes, changes of costume and make-up or the old-fashioned device of watching the hands of a clock moving.

In Paul Greengrass's brilliantly filmed *The Bourne Supremacy* (2004) Matt Damon shifts from Goa, Berlin, Moscow, Naples and Amsterdam in cinematic speed that would afford him millions of air miles. Most common in film is to show a shift in time as a cut or a dissolve to the next scene. Equally, a montage sequence can show shift of time. If we were to represent movement in film in real time, everything would seem incredibly long, but we have come to accept the convention of temporal shifts in film.

Stanley Kubrick is the master of time shifts and in 2001: *A Space Odyssey* he plays with narrative structure by opening the film with the apes throwing a bone and cuts to a space ship a thousand years later.

Real time has become an interesting dynamic in the popular television series *24*, with each episode showing a 24-hour period in the life of Jack Bauer who works for the American Government. This, of course, is not a new dynamic.

The Film, *High Noon* (1952, directed by Fred Zinnerman with Gary Cooper and a very young Grace Kelly) was innovative for its time, as the story unfolds in approximate real time from 10.40 to high noon in an eighty-four minute film. Several shots of clocks are prominent throughout the film and they correspond with actual minutes ticking unlike the device of moving clocks to show time passing.

The long tracking shot with no cuts also allows the camera to follow a character in real time. It is beloved of filmmakers such as the late Robert Altman in *The Player*, Martin Scorsese in *Raging Bull*, Stanley Kubrick in *The Shining*, Oliver Stone in everything and other auteur directors who are known for their use of these more documentary, realistic techniques. The effect of the long take is that the audience is kept involved, as cuts can be jarring.

Temporal shifts in theatre can also be dramatic. Time in theatre is live, but there are leaps of time, one of the longest being the sixteen-year gap in *The Winter's Tale*. Time can be dealt with by changes in acts/blackouts, curtains. Broadway moves from time to time with the speed of revolving sets. The Greek /(Ibsenite) unity of time (twenty-four hours) still remains a theatrical convention that allows for a theatrical compression and an explosion of discovery. The actual time of a play, of course, varies. A play can be anywhere from the usual two and a half hours to Beckett's play, *Breath*, which takes thirty seconds.

Arthur Miller's *The Death of a Salesman* or Brian Friel's *Philadelphia Here I Come*, Tennessee Williams's *Glass Menagerie*, all use 'cinematic' techniques to give us time that is not causal. The present and the past are presented simultaneously through the use of apron as neutral space or through a narrator.

The flashback to capture past time is a device used in both film and the theatre. In theatre, time is often dealt with through flashback, narration, prologues, and the well-known device of the 'voice- over'. Most sources still credit D.W. Griffith with the introduction of the flashback device, particularly in *Intolerance* (1916). There are parallel plotlines happening in different time periods, all around the theme of intolerance through the ages.

Films with complicated flashbacks can upset the 'simple reality' of the filmgoer and cause confusion. A film like *Memento* (2000) with Guy Pearce, or *The Prestige* (2006) with Christian Bale, both directed by Christopher Nolan, make brilliant use of flashback scenes, because memory is central to their themes. *The Eternal Sunshine of the Spotless Mind* is another film, by Charlie Kaufman, where the laws of time and space are constantly broken. *Citizen Kane* (Orson Welles, 1941) depended hugely on the flashback to show the character of Charles Foster Kane's life out of sequence, giving different characters' viewpoints. *Casablanca* (Michael Curtiz, 1942) uses the flashback to reveal specific character memories.

Connected to time, the dynamic of duration is important. Duration is part of what makes some great modern plays work on stage, but not on film, as we will see with Beckett's plays such as *Endgame* or a play such as O'Neill's *Long Day's Journey Into Night*. Eugene O'Neill's *Long Day's Journey* allows the audience to experience the discomfiture of the long day's journey almost in real time.

Robert Brustein observed: I believe that his style (the long, dense interior drama) is actually meant to create a different theatrical context in which the audience experiences things in time ... Should we stage it realistically or as O'Neill himself said, 'holding the old family Kodak up to ill-nature?' Should we present it in real time, at the risk of alienating our audience?[9]

On film, these plays often fail because they don't make the audience uncomfortable enough with the duration of waiting: *Synecdoche*, the new film directed by writer Charlie Kaufman (of *Being John Malkovich* fame), manages to create that sense of duration, partly because it is a play within a film and uses the syntax of theatre.

The Dynamic of the Audience

The contrast between film and theatre in audience and audience experience is a central dynamic. Some say that film appeals to a mass audience while the theatre attracts an elite minority audience. Throughout history, theatre, of course, appealed at times to a public audience and at times to a more private audience. With the introduction of the sound film, the movies became the main mass audience art form before television took over.

Does an audience view theatre and cinema in the same way? With theatre, the audience gets dressed up, usually spends a good deal of money (a considerable amount for a Broadway production). It is a public event. Drinks are ordered before the play begins in anticipation of the interval. In the theatre, the audience gathers in groups and waits for curtain time. The auditorium is more brightly lit during the performance than a movie theatre is and absorption in the drama is periodically broken by intermissions and scene changes. During the performance the audience member must actively suspend disbelief since even the most realist productions require the acceptance of a number of obvious conventions, and must actively participate in choosing what to look at, since the entire stage is ordinarily in view.

The cinema on the other hand is less expensive, though adding the price of popcorn, drink, etc., can make the experience costly. The movie audience enters singly in small groups and even annoyingly at any point in the film. The film audience is more isolated in darkness and focused on a large cinema screen. Part of the film experience is the escapism of surrendering to the film, only seeing what the director has chosen to show you.

A central and obvious difference in the dynamic of film and theatre audience is that actors who perform in a film are not in contact with their audience. One is relieved of the tension which comes with the performances by live actors who might, for example, fluff their lines. In theatre the audience affects a performance and actors. This doesn't happen in film where tonality is predetermined before an audience goes to the cinema. The audience always adds an extra dimension and affects performance.

Yet, noisy, moving, popcorn-crunching audiences can affect the enjoyment of a film. Equally, a dark print or an 'out-of-synch' soundtrack can interfere with the experience of the cinema audience.

The Dynamic of Distance and Space

The relation of the audience to the stage or screen is a central dynamic. In film, the audience is guided through the camera's eye. The Cinematographer or Director of Photography is the one who manages this dynamic. Directors such as the great Stanley Kubrick tightly control this view. The Hungarian filmmaker, theorist Bela Balazs commented: 'Theatre always maintains its action in a spatial continuity, stable distance from the spectator and one unchanged angle.'[10]

In film, both the distance and the angle from which we see the action can change through camera angle, level, height, distance, how far away or close up the camera is from the action. A long shot, a mid shot, a close up, an establishing shot, a point of view shot, a wide angle shot, a two shot, a soft focus all mediate meaning.

We know that the realists in cinema favoured the more objective deep focus, long shot and static camera, while the so called formalists preferred the more subjective shallow focus, close-up and moving camera. The movements of the camera, be it a zoom in a pan, a tracking shot, or hand- held camera, all have their own grammar of purpose.

The camera distance affects how we respond to the action and our degree of involvement. We may engage with the main actor of a film because of the intimacy of the number of close-ups or through the use of hand-held camera.

In the theatre, the spectator is usually fixed in one position viewing the acting from a constant position and point of view. Theatre doesn't do close-ups unless you are seated in a box near the stage or on the stage.

In the cinema, although spectators remains physically in their seats, perception is constantly changing the perspective, moving in upon the action, moving back from it, seeing it from the position of one of the characters or seen from a position impossible in real experience.

But theatre can use some of the same tools as the cinematographer. The Theatre of the '60s of Happenings, group involvement etc. changed our relationship to the fixed seat of the audience looking on to the action. The work of Jerzy Grotowski sought to break down the line between the presenter and the presented. Augusto Boal describes the spect-actor as the dual role of spectator and actor in his Forum Theatre.

Antonin Artaud with his Theatre of Cruelty wanted a more intimate relationship between performer and audience. He wanted to 'abolish the stage and the auditorium and replace them by a single site, without partition or barrier of any kind. Where the spectator and the spectacle between the actor and the spectator is engulfed.'[11]

Brecht also wanted a relationship between actor and audience as dialectic where the audience would not suspend belief as it does in a cinema, but would function as critical observer.

Beckerman argues that in the Elizabethan theatre there were different types of audience intimacy in the public playhouses. In the private theatres, the cavaliers often shared the space with the performers. In the court theatres, during the performance of the masque, the presentation space remained isolated during the first part of the presentation (the anti masque); then as the dance began, the performers invited certain of the spectators to enter the dancers' circle and in effect become performers.

From the beginnings of cinema, film-makers have used subjective vision, distorting and emphasizing, if necessary, the visual process. They shoot out of focus to show the vision of a drunk or the point of view of the driver. Filmmakers wanted to show and make the viewer feel what the character feels through the camera lens.

An example of this is in Woody Allen's comedy *Deconstructing Harry* (1997) where the character played by Robin Williams feels out of sorts, 'sort of fuzzy.' Allen, for unusual comic effect, deliberately films the actor out of focus while the rest of the cast remain in focus.

In Arthur Miller's *Death of a Salesman* (1949), Willy Loman says 'I'm feeling kind of temporary', The play, originally called *Inside His Head*, reveals a man cracking up, literally going out of focus on stage. Miller experimented with the subjective reality using the direction of Elia Kazan and the design of Jo Melziner to capture this temporary and out-of-focus feeling. Miller describes his play as subjective realism.

The Dynamic of Realism

The most difficult dynamic to tackle, but perhaps the most pertinent to the topic of holding the mirror up to nature, is the dynamic of realism. Because of film's origins in the photographic, we associate it with an art that records.

Film grew up when stage realism was at is height. Because film could do realism better, theatre had to move away from the photographic to the more plastic theatre, as Williams calls it in his important *Preface to The Glass Menagerie* (1949). Theatre found new realisms by exploring the lenses of Expressionism and later other experimentalisms in the work of Strindberg, of Brecht, Pirandello, Beckett, Pinter and others. And just as painting and the novel had shed the function of mimesis to film so did the stage. By the late '20s, the avant-garde theatre was able to challenge film. Except for the period beginning with Ibsen and the movement of realism and naturalism, theatre was never really a theatre of naturalness.

Alardyce Nicoll suggests that the screen gives the illusion of actuality itself. The screen actor is not taught to act. He is himself and the argument runs, rightly so, since the screen must seem to be life itself. Such is the power of the camera.

Eric Bentley questions this:

> ... Audiences [don't] believe that what happens on the screen is really happening or that it has happened – at least no more than theatre audiences do. After all, it was in the theater that the proverbial man in the gallery told Othello to leave the lady

alone, and it was on the radio that the announcement of the end of the world was taken literally. [12]

Truth vs illusion is one of theatre's greatest themes from *Oedipus Rex* to Calderon's *Life is a Dream* right up to contemporary theatre. Tom Wingfield in Williams's *The Glass Menagerie* reveals the magic of theatre: 'Yes, I have tricks in my pocket, I have things up my sleeve. But I am the very opposite of a stage magician. He gives you illusion that has the appearance of truth. I give you truth in the pleasing disguise of illusion.'

The Dynamic of Alive vs. Celluloid

Theatre is not cinema because it is live. There are real people in front of you. There is a tension, a presence, a spontaneity, a conflict that film can never match. Theatre is three-dimensional, film is two-dimensional. In the theatre we see a performance being created as we watch it. In film, we have to forget that this is a performance that has taken place in the past.

Cate Blanchett said in the same interview quoted earlier: 'What's great about the theatre is at least every night you get the chance to go out and re-offend.' (*Guardian* 13/1/07).

Depending on your budget, a film can be shot endlessly and put together in the editing suite. A play goes on and there is no going back once the performance has started, except the next night when the performance is new. It is strange then that film can feel more real than theatre. Apart from the moments when the sound is out of 'synch' with the movement of the actor's lips, little else can go wrong. Actors' performances change from night to night in the theatre. In film they are fixed. In the theatre anything can go wrong – from illness, even death of an actor to the forgetting of lines.

Famously, Ralph Fiennes in a recent Dublin production of *Faith Healer* came out of character to berate the owner of a mobile phone which went off in the front row. Audiences have witnessed open flies, costumes falling off and sets falling down at a crucial moment. If the door-flat falls down in Ibsen's *A Doll's House*, at the moment that the slam is meant to be heard around the world, the result is farce.

Yet there is a strange dynamic with film, in that you can see the same film several times and yet see it differently: A film's reception is affected by one's moods, one's company, one's seat, tiredness. A film is different, depending on the age at which you see it. Film is mutable.

The Dynamic of the Communal:

Drama is a communal art involving a group of performers and a larger group who watch the performance. A film is watched by a group, some who arrive after the film has started and leave before the credits finish. A film festival is the closest we come to the communal in film where a group gather to watch types of films such as horror films.

Our communal sense is being eroded by new technology. Many people now relax in their own homes and watch a DVD rather than go out to the cinema and pay for a baby-sitter and parking. The new digital technology allows us to programme films in advance and to create our own schedule of TV programmes and films.

In days of yore, there used to be discussions in staff rooms about a film or programme shown the night before. Those 'water-cooler' films and programmes are disappearing because of the rise of the new technology of watching film and television. The days of sharing the watching of a programme or indeed the Christmas movie are long over. Most people have already seen the Christmas film on DVD or it is on each day on Sky Movies for a week!

Our viewing experience, influenced by MTV and SKY, has challenged how people consume images and has altered how we receive narrative. Instead of the communal experience, viewers can now watch a movie on iPods on a bus, a TV programme on a playbox. You can download and upgrade. Young people can watch programmes and films on screens as small as their mobile phones which hardly can be shared There is simply more product. What Patrick Mason called the MBA reductionism.

One of the greatest differences then is that theatre still retains some of the communal experience that was at the heart of its origins in the religious festivals of Dionysus.

The Dynamic of Metatheatre and Metacinema

We experience the cinema in a state of double consciousness, an astonishing phenomenon where the illusion of reality is inseparable from the awareness that it is really an illusion.[13]

If presentational theatre does not let the audience forget they are viewing a play and metafiction does not let the readers forget they are reading a book, a metafilm does not let the audience forget that they are watching a film. Metafilm is a kind of film that self-consciously addresses the devices of film.

Singin' in the Rain (Gene Kelly and Stanley Donen, 1952) is one of the many great movies about movie, a film within a film with a great deal of filmic intertextuality. One of the comic ironies is that Debby Reynolds (Kathy Selden), who is dubbing for Jean Hagen (the Lina Lamont character), was actually dubbed herself with the voice of Betty Noyes for most of the numbers.

Movie stars also affect our perceptions of actor and character in a metacinematic way. In Levinson's *Rainman*, (1988) Dustin Hoffman is recognized as a well-known actor and at the same time is accepted as the autistic character, Raymond Babbitt. Equally, Leonardo Di Caprio in Lasse Hallstrom's *What's Eating Gilbert Grape* (1993) evades his image as a heartthrob by our double awareness that this is a well-known actor playing the part of Arnie Grape. This double consciousness is what sometimes causes a director to look for an unknown actor to play a part, so that it may be realized with integrity and truthfulness.

The Play Within a Play

Samuel Beckett calls attention to play as play, and Shakespeare uses a play within a play to heighten our meta-theatrical awareness. In theatre, there is always a double awareness that there is a character and an actor present. When we watch an actor sword-fighting on stage, we may fear for the character's life, but we are also aware of the skill of the actor.

Most directors 'open up a play' when they turn it into a film, to adapt it to the new medium and prevent it looking too stagey or static. While most films have interior and exterior scenes, many plays are confined to the four walls of a single setting.

Stanley Kaufmann says that one of the great strengths of drama is its power to charge a confined space with emotional meaning. A theatrically necessary feeling of claustrophobia can be lost if the play is opened up too much and the drama lost. There are important exceptions such as a film like *Glengarry Glen Ross*. Mike Figgis in his film version of Strindberg's *Miss Julie* (1999) interestingly opens up the film to the outside (though the play remains indoors).

In 2001, Michael Colgan, Artistic Director of the Gate Theatre in Dublin and film maker Alan Moloney, produced a Beckett Film Festival – all nineteen of Beckett's stage plays (minus *Eleuthéria*), to be treated as films by well-known directors.

Beckett himself was intensely interested in and well read about film. Throughout the late 1920s and 1930s he regularly went to the cinema in Paris and London. In 1936, Beckett wrote to the great Russian filmmaker Eisenstein to apply for entry to the Moscow State School of Cinematography:

> I have no experience of studio work and it is naturally in the scenario and editing of the subject that I am most interested. It is because I realize that the script is a function of the means of realization that I am anxious to make contact with your mastery of these and beg you to consider me a serious cineaste worthy of admission to your school. (Anna McMullan, *The Irish Times*, 2/2/2001.)

It was 1936, so Eisenstein probably never saw the letter. Beckett remained fascinated by film medium and in 1964 wrote and directed a short film called *Film with Buster Keaton*. Didi and Gogo are often considered direct descendants of Laurel and Hardy whom Beckett loved, along with the silent films of Charlie Chaplin.

Of the nineteen films, some use the grammar and syntax of cinema to breathe a new dimension into Beckett's writing, where others clearly miss the point. They remain an interesting experiment that show some of the differences in the dynamic of theatre-making and film-making. Some of the shorter plays are more amenable to adaptation to film than their longer, more critically celebrated companion pieces: the stolid duration of waiting for a *Godot* or for *Endgame* to end, is lost on screen.

The length of the longer plays depends on a certain discomfiture in the audience, a condition to which many lines refer: (*Endgame*) 'This is slow work; This is not much fun; This is deadly; Do you not think this has gone on long enough?' (*Waiting for Godot*): 'Nothing happens, nobody comes, nobody goes, this is awful.'

In Conor McPherson's filmic version of *Endgame*, there is no real attempt to translate the play into film. It is a competently shot record of an ordinary performance What is gained is simply what cinema itself makes possible – the precision of the close-up, the ability to change the perspective of the viewer so it seems at times to be that of one of the actors.

Fintan O'Toole, principal drama critic for *The Irish Times*, suggests the problem is with the adaptation of Beckett's humour. The cinematic *Endgame* is less funny:

> One of the funniest moments in *Endgame* is when Clov takes his telescope and instead of looking out the windows as he does at intervals through the play, points it directly into the

auditorium. Asked what he sees, he replies: 'A multitude in transports of delight.'

On screen, an actor cannot look at the audience. Instead Clov looks through the telescope at Hamm and the line ceases to make sense and the joke is lost.

Patricia Rozema's film version of *Happy Days* sticks closely to Beckett's lines and movements and Rosaleen Linehan recreates her stage performance at the Gate Theatre. Rozema makes one huge change, by placing the action in a real filmed landscape of sky, mountain and stone instead of the mound of earth that entombs the character of Winnie. This might seem like a rather obvious thing to do in film, but it interferes quite radically with the nature of the piece.

Beckett wrote to American friend and director Alan Schneider:

> what should characterize the whole scene, sky and earth, is a pathetic unsuccessful realism, that kind of tawdriness you get in third rate musical or pantomime ... laughably earnest bad imitation.'[14]

In Peter Brook's production in Paris (1963) with Madeline Renaud and Louis Barrault, the most exciting and theatrical moment is when Winnie's umbrella magically combusts on stage. The amazed audience gasp 'How did they do that?' The strangeness and wonder of theatre is lost in the film because cinema can do this magic with discontinuous shots.

Beckett's plays are best produced in a void, with the sense that nothing is out there beyond the stage set except backstage. Beckett's plays make self-conscious reference to the fact that we are in a play and that there is an audience.

> **Hamm**: An aside ape. Did you never hear of an aside?
> More complications. Not an underplot I trust ...
> **Clov**: This is called making an exit.

It is strange then that film can feel more real than theatre. Perhaps it is because it is closest to surface reality, the photographic, or maybe because it is closest to our dreams and subconscious and filtered through our imagination.

If melodrama is cinema's first cousin, we must listen to Eric Bentley who described melodrama as the naturalism of the dream life. Melodrama is more like pure escapism, more like film. Our dreams are more like action films where things explode, there are chases, and big events.[15]

Subversion in cinema starts when the theatre darkens and the screen lights up. For the cinema is a place of magic where psychological and environmental factors combine to create an openness to wonder and suggestion, and unlocking of the unconscious. It is a shrine at which modern rituals rooted in atavistic memories and subconscious desires are acted out in darkness and seclusion from the outer world.[16]

In a recent interview, Lillete Dubey, a well known Indian theatre and film personality, brought out her sense of difference between theatre and film:

> In a play, you can act like a man or a woman, a nine-year-old or a ninety-year-old. You can do anything, and people will believe you. You can create a look, an ambience and your audience will believe you. That's why you feel like a king on stage. (http://www.radiosargam.)

David Fincher's recent film *The Curious Case of Benjamin Button* did all of that, collecting several technical academy awards along the way. Is there anything then that theatre does that film cannot?

Daniel Katz, a young film maker and recent convert to theatre, said in a conference call from New York:

> Theatre has one great distinction over film, it is live, the startling experience of existing at every new moment, and that is its enduring magic.

Bibliography

Arnheim, Rudolf, *Film as Art* (Berkeley: University of California Press, 1957).

Artaud, Antonin, *The Theater and its Double* (New York: Grove Press, 1958).

Bailey, J.O. ed., *British Plays of the 19th Century* (New York: Odyssey, 1966).

Balazs, Bela, *Theory of the Film* (New York: Roy Publishers, 1953).

Bentley, Eric. *The Life of the Drama*. New York: Atheneum, 1964.

Beckerman, Bernard. *Dynamics of Drama Theory and Method of Analysis* (New York: Drama Book Specialists, 1979).

Blok (quoted in Jay Ledya, *Kino: A History of the Russian and Soviet Film* (London: George Allen and Unwin, 1960,) 130, in Hurt.

Brook, Peter, *The Empty Space* (New York: Discuss Books, 1968).

Harmon, Maurice, ed., *No Author Better Served* (Cambridge: Harvard University Press, 1998).

Hurt, James, ed., *Focus on Film and Theatre* (New Jersey: Prentice-Hall Inc. 1974).

McMullan, Anna. *The Irish Times*, February 2, 2001, 'Fascinated by Film' (Beckett)

Monaco, James, *How to Read a Film*, 3rd Edition. (New York: Oxford University Press, 2000).

Morin, Edgar, *The Cinema or the Imaginary Man* (Minneapolis: University of Minnesota Press, 2005).

O'Toole, Fintan, *The Irish Times* Reviews.

Schultz, David G., *The Chicago Survey*, http://chicago-survey.blogspot.com/2006/09/long-days-journey-into-night.html

Toulet, Emmanuelle, *Cinema is 100 Years Old* (London: Thames and Hudson. 1995).

Vardac, A. Nicholas, *Stage to Screen, Theatrical Origins of Early Film: David Garrick to D.W. Griffith* (New York: Da Capo, 1987).

Vogel, Amos, *Film as a Subversive Art* (New York: Art Publishers 1974

Willett, John, *Brecht on Theatre* (London: Methuen, 1984).

Woody Allen, *Deconstructing Harry*, 1997.

(http://www.radiosargam.com/films/archives/9132/theatre-or-cinema-lillete-brings-the-difference.html)

DVDs

Early Cinema, Primitives and Pioneers, BFI Video Publishing, Producer Adrian Raistrick (Lumiere and Melies)

Singing in the Rain, Times Warner Company, 1952, Director Stanley Donen and Gene Kelly.

Beckett on Film, DVD Blue Angel Films, Tyrone Productions, 2001.

---

[1] James Hurt, *Focus on Film and Theatre* (New Jersey, 1974), 130.

[2] Peter Brook, *The Empty Space*, 9.

[3] James Hurt, *Focus on Film and Theatre*, 8.

[4] Robert Arnheim, *Film as Art*, 17.

[5] A. Nicholas Vardac, *Stage to Screen,* xvii.

[6] J.O.Bailey (ed.), *British Plays of the Nineteenth Century*, 7.

[7] Antonin Artaud, *The Theater and Its Double*, 37.

[8] Hurt, *Focus on Film and Theatre*, 10.

[9] David G. Schulz, *The Chicago Survey* (http://chicago-survey.blogspot.com/2006/09/long-days-journey-into-night.html)

---

[10] Bela Balazs, *Theory of the Film* (New York, 1953), 44.

[11] Artaud, *The Theater and Its Double*, 96.

[12] Hurt, *Focus on Film and Theatre*, 54.

[13] Edgar Morin, *The Cinema or The Imaginary Man*, 8.

[14] Maurice Harmon (ed.), *No Author Better Served*, 91.

[15] Eric Bentley, *The Life of the Drama*, 205.

[16] Amos Vogel, *Film as a Subversive Art*, 1974.

6 | like a bell with many echoes: drama and opera

John Buckley

It is a great honour to have been asked to give the final lecture in the current series of Seamus Heaney Lectures and I am grateful to the organizing committee for their kind invitation. I am especially thankful to Dr Pat Burke for his suggestion that I speak about my chamber opera *The Words Upon the Window-Pane* and its relationship to the Yeats play on which it is based.[1] I am further indebted to Pat for suggesting the wonderfully evocative title of the lecture 'like a bell with many echoes'. My title is taken from Yeats's own introduction to *The Words Upon the Window-Pane* and seems wholly appropriate for a drama in which memory, recollection, echo and resonance exercise such prominent roles.

Drama and all forms of music, but especially opera, are best experienced in performance. As Oliver Taplin writes, 'The text is no more than a transcript, a scenario. The play's the thing',[2] as Hamlet says. The same can be said of the musical score. While text and score undoubtedly have intrinsic value as literature, it is how they are transformed and realized through performance that is of interest to me here. In drama and opera, gesture, expression, tone of voice, physical posture, subtle nuances of timing and emphasis, are not added in narrative form as they are of necessity in a novel, but embody an essential element of the experience. Drama and music unfold and can only be experienced through time. In a very real sense the canvas of the dramatist and composer does not so much consist of words and musical sounds, as it does of time. It is through the control and manipulation of time with the words or the music that the art is created and experienced.

There can be few artistic endeavours, whose origin may be as accurately located in terms of place and time as that of opera. The genre is a direct product of the deliberations and speculations of the late sixteenth-century Florentine Camerata. Under the initial patronage of Count Giovanni Bardi, and later that of Jacopo Corsi, groups of intellectuals, consisting of musicians, writers, philosophers and others, organized a series of meetings to deliberate on the nature of literature, science and the arts.

These meetings took place in a period of extraordinary artistic and intellectual ferment in Florence. As the cultural birthplace of the Italian Renaissance, Florence in the fifteenth century had established itself as the leading centre of artistic, humanistic, technological and scientific endeavour. The patronage of the Medici family, the *de facto* rulers of Florence for the best part of two centuries, led to an extraordinary blossoming in the arts and sciences. To have been the patron of Botticelli, or Michaelangelo or Leonardo, would be sufficient to earn any patron the gratitude of posterity; the Medicis were patrons of all three. Much of the imaginative genius of the period was fired by the rediscovery and purchase of rare classical manuscripts and artefacts. The development of the first public libraries further enhanced the role of Florence as a leading centre in the advancement of the liberal arts.

Amongst the ambitions of the Florentine Camerata was an attempt to restore and reclaim the glories of ancient Greek drama. As no notation of the music associated with Greek drama was available, and with no clear idea as to how it sounded, the Camerata based its conclusions on written accounts and on speculation. These included the belief that the words of ancient Greek tragedy were sung or at least declaimed throughout the entire performance to heighten the emotional expression. This combination of speech and music was thought to be an embodiment of the ancient Greek style.

In his essay *Seneca in Elizabethan Translations*, T.S. Eliot offers a concise and perceptive insight to ancient Greek theatre: Behind the dialogue of Greek drama we are always conscious of a concrete visual actuality, and behind that of a specific emotional actuality. Behind the drama of words is the drama of action, the timbre of voice and voice, the uplifted hand or tense muscle and the particular emotion.[3] Words, action and emotion are fused into one experience. In opera, all of these elements – the dialogue, the visual actualities and the emotional actualities – lie behind and are at the same time embedded in and articulated through the music. The music is both the immediate surface experience and simultaneously, the deepest core of opera. In common with Greek drama, opera presents a continuous dramatic representation of human interaction, with the intent of an emotional appeal and connection to the audience.

The early Italian term for opera was 'dramma per musica'; drama through music, and this resonant description elegantly captures the intimate fusion of music, dialogue and action that the form embodies. In the new art form, the text had to be audible and intelligible and follow the natural rhythmic patterns of speech declamation, all of which led to a syllabic style of word setting. Especially emotive words could be embellished with a variety of ornamentation or given an elaborate melismatic[4] treatment. Instrumental accompaniment provided the possibility of expressive and descriptive harmony: the use of dissonance for distress, falling motifs for sighs and sadness, upward scales and figurations for jubilation, and so forth.

Early operas were written for the entertainment of an elite courtly audience. In this they could have hardly differed more from their source in Greek drama, with its formal structures, stylized sense of ritual and public dimension or mass social phenomenon[5] to use Paul Cartledge's phrase. Nonetheless, the concept of Greek drama, especially tragedy, played a crucial element in the origins of opera. It was in attempting to recreate the past that the radically new art form of opera was invented.

More immediate Italian antecedents of opera include the intermedi, entertainments performed by singers, actors and dancers in costume usually based on a pastoral or mythological theme and inserted between the acts of plays, with which they frequently had no connection. The lavish spectacle of these entertainments played an important role in the growing popularity of opera, following the opening of the first public opera house in Venice in 1637.

Appropriately enough, the earliest surviving operas all draw on ancient Greek myths and legends for their subject matter. The first surviving opera is *Euridice* with a libretto by Ottavio Rinuccini and music by Jacopo Peri, both regular members of the Florentine Camerata. The first performance of *Euridice* was given in 1600 as part of the wedding celebrations of Maria de' Medici and King Henry IV of France.

Rinnucini and Peri had collaborated some years earlier on another similar work *Dafne*, but the music was never published and as a result only a few fragments exist.

These early attempts at opera are important as they exemplify the new musical approach: monodic[6] and declamatory in style and representing a marked contrast to the contrapuntal[7] complexity of the earlier polyphonic music of Palestrina and his contemporaries. In a sense, these works are a testing ground for the new style; in Rinuccini's words to show what our new music could do.

Within the remarkably short space of seven years, opera had produced its first indubitable masterpiece, *L'Orfeo, favola in Musica*, Orpheus, a story or fable in music, with a libretto by Allesandro Striggio and music by Claudio Monteverdi, one of the greatest and most influential composers in the history of music. As Leslie Orrey writes in *A Concise History of Opera*:

> Peri and Caccini were no more than competent practitioners, and something else was needed if these ventures were to be raised beyond the level of interesting experiments ... The time was ripe for a miracle – a word that is hardly too strong for 'L'Orfeo'[8]

The first performance of *L'Orfeo* was given almost exactly four hundred years ago on February 24, 1607 in a small room at the ducal palace of the Gonzaga family in Mantua. No expense was spared in the preparations for the opera, and without a doubt the artistic rivalry of the Florentine and Mantuan courts played a major role here. The greatest singers and instrumentalists of the day were hired and exhaustively rehearsed, the libretto was printed and distributed to an audience of connoisseurs, somewhat akin to our own assembly here this evening.

An outstanding though perhaps in some regards obvious characteristic of early operas is that they all feature legendary musicians as heroes, namely the god Apollo and in particular, his son Orpheus. Monteverdi's great masterpiece *L'Orfeo* is above all an opera about the expressive power of music. In ancient Greek legend, Orpheus was the archetypal musician. Such was the power of his music that he could charm and soothe the wild beasts; make rocks and trees to dance, make the winds to pause and even cause rivers to arrest and change course. The power of music in Monteverdi's opera is, however, even greater and enables Orpheus to cross the river Styx and restore his beloved Eurydice to life. Eurydice can hardly complain at her final demise; it is only Orfeo's concern and love that causes him to turn around and thus consign Eurydice for ever to the underworld.

The prologue of *L'Orfeo* introduces us to La Musica, the allegorical characterization of music, who talks of its expressive power and of Orfeo's amazing skills. Her five stanzas are separated by an orchestral ritornello or refrain. The fifth stanza summarizes:

> Now while I change my songs, now happy, now sad,
> Let no small bird stir among these trees,
> No noisy waves be heard on these river-banks,
> And let each little breeze halt in its course.

The beautiful orchestral refrain or ritornello reappears at various points throughout the opera, especially where music and its magical powers are evoked. The concept of the orchestra developed as a direct consequence of the birth of opera. In ancient Greek theatre, the orchestra was the large circular area between the performing space and the audience. The chorus, usually a group of fifteen, normally entered the orchestra after the opening scene and remained there for the rest of the play. Its main function was to dance and sing or chant the choral odes, which act as a structural device in separating the acts of the drama. The dancing was clearly important: the word 'orchestra' actually means the dancing place. The chorus was accompanied by a single musician, playing an aulos, a type of reedpipe, with two diverging branches.

As the musicians who accompanied the singers in early operas also sat in the area between the performers and the audience, they and the space they occupied were referred to as the orchestra. It was only in the eighteenth century that the term came to be exclusively used for the group of musicians. Monteverdi's orchestra for *L'Orfeo* specifies a wide range of instruments, including woodwinds, strings, brass, drums and a range of chord-playing instruments. This sounds very like an embryonic version of our modern symphony orchestra. The music however is not orchestrated in the sense of particular parts of the music being assigned to specific instruments and it is likely that the listed instruments were simply those that happened to be available at Mantua. The clear characterization of the music however suggests that brass and timpani be used for fanfares and toccatas[9], strings for more lyrical passages, and recorders for pastoral scenes, and this is generally the approach taken in modern productions of the opera.

The role of the Greek chorus was entirely different to that of a chorus in opera. The members of Greek chorus were not central participants in the drama: they were more like commentators contemplating universal truths. When not performing, the chorus remained motionless. As Oliver Taplin says in his seminal study *Greek Tragedy in Action*:

> It is the place of choral song (in Greek tragedy) to move into a different world, a different register, distinct from the specific events of the plot. The lyrics are not tied down in place and time, in language, in the reasoned sequence of speech and thought, as the dialogue is: they swerve through a sequence of associative, often emotional links to a highly coloured world of more wide-ranging, universal and abstract trains of thought.[10]

The choruses of the operatic repertoire are in contrast, active participants in the drama, such as slaves, soldiers, pilgrims, shepherds and so forth. They provide a backdrop for the main characters and also present the composer with opportunities for stirring and memorable set pieces.

It is clear that in essence, opera consists of a fusion – words, music and action. Song writers as well as opera composers frequently find themselves having to answer the question: Which comes first, the words or the music? Sammy Cahn, lyricist of innumerable popular songs such as 'Let it Snow, Let it Snow, Let it Snow' and 'Love and Marriage' said that neither words nor music came first; the telephone call always came first! The answer of Ira Gershwin, brother of George and lyricist of many of his greatest songs, was even more forthright, saying that the contract always came first. In whatever order, and with or without preliminaries, words and music must come together if we are to have opera.

The little book of the text, the libretto, usually precedes the music though the two are frequently developed in tandem. The relationship between librettist and composer can often be elaborate and complex. Correspondence between Verdi and Arrigo Boito, the librettist of *Otello*, vividly portrays the process of collaboration. Boito's letter of August 1881 in response to requests from Verdi contains the following:

> I shall add four lines for Roderigo. Perhaps the other four for Desdemona will not be needed. It's so true that a silent Otello is grander and more terrible that my opinion would be not to have him speak at all during the whole ensemble ... After the ensemble, and after the words, 'Tutti fuggite Otello', it seems to me that Otello does not speak or cry out enough. He is silent for four lines, and it seems to me that (scenically speaking,) after

'Che d'ogni senso il priva', Otello ought to bellow out one or two lines: 'Away! I detest you, myself, the whole world!' – And it seems to me that a few lines could be spared, when Otello and Iago remain together.[11]

Many composers choose to write their own librettos, but more frequently the process involves collaboration with an established writer. The libretto can be based on an original scenario or can adapt an existing story or play. The latter usually involves a severe reduction of the original text, a stripping of the play to its essentials. On a purely practical basis, it takes longer to sing a text than it does to speak it. In reference to Boito's libretto for *Otello*, Charles Osborne In his book *The Complete Operas of Verdi* goes so far as to claim that:

> It is formally more attractive than Shakespeare's original, not least because its structure in four uninterrupted acts is more compact than Shakespeare's rambling five-act division into fifteen scenes. Boito dispenses with Shakespeare's Act 1, thus allowing his four acts to take place on Cyprus. The Venetian Senate is no great loss.[12]

Strong words indeed, but Verdi's powerfully dramatic music compensates for any reduction in the original text, and places the opera at the zenith of the genre.

It is time to turn to *The Words Upon the Window-Pane*. In placing my own chamber opera after a discussion of Monteverdi and Verdi, I hope you don't think that in some misguided way, I regard it as a belated apotheosis of the operatic genre! In his introduction, Yeats refers to 'My little play, *The Words Upon the Window-Pane*'. My little opera *The Words Upon the Window-Pane* lasts a mere twenty minutes and has a small cast and orchestra. Nonetheless, even a twenty-minute chamber opera doesn't suddenly materialize from thin air. It has to be conceived and composed and I will now elaborate on that process.

My chamber opera *The Words Upon the Window-Pane* began with neither words, music, contract or even telephone call, but rather more mundanely, and in keeping with our bureaucratic times, it began with an application form.

To mark the occasion of Dublin becoming the European City of Culture in 1991, Opera Theatre Company invited applications from composers and, as a result commissioned four chamber operas. All four operas were to be performed in one production and have as a common thread, a connection to Dublin. The four operas were *The Poet and his Double,* a confrontation in four scenes, with a prologue and epilogue: text and music by Raymond Deane; *Hot Food with Strangers*: text by Judy Cravis and music by Marion Ingoldsby; *Position Seven*: text by James Conway and music by Kenneth Chalmers; and *The Words Upon the Window-Pane* with a libretto by Hugh Maxton, adapted from the play by William Butler Yeats and music by John Buckley.

I would like to put this imaginative approach of Opera Theatre Company into context. It is hardly an exaggeration to say that as a nation, Ireland is not at the forefront of international developments in opera. Dublin shares a dubious distinction with Nicosia and Valetta as being the only EU capital cities, without an opera house and/or a permanent professional large-scale opera company. Imagine Dublin without a National Theatre, National Library, National Gallery or a National Museum, yet we don't have a National Opera House and in fact have only had a National Concert Hall for the past twenty-five years. Many moderately sized European cities, such as Cardiff, Reykjavik, Vilnius, Mannheim or Cluz Napoca in Romania, all boast opera houses and companies.

Against this background, Opera Theatre Company has displayed an imaginative approach to the commissioning and productions of new operas. A new cast and team is assembled for each production and the focus is on chamber opera: a small cast, a small accompanying ensemble, minimal sets and props and so forth. The specifications of the commission of *The Words Upon the Window-Pane* were far removed from the extravagant dimensions of the nineteenth century concept of grand opera. The cast could consist of a maximum of six specified voices, the orchestra or chamber ensemble of seven specified instruments, and the duration should not exceed twenty minutes.

If these limitations seem severe, they are in fact on the contrary, a type of blessing to any composer. All art aspires to precision of expression and the restrictions imposed by the circumstances of the commission of the opera, conversely lent a sense of freedom. In Stravinsky's succinct phrase the more art is controlled, limited, worked over, the more it is free.[13] An almost overwhelming number of possibilities offer themselves to the composer at every moment of a composition and it is only by narrowing the field of options that any progress whatsoever can be made. Any hope of achieving an organic, coherent, and stylistically consistent work depends on the composer's ability to choose and, equally importantly, discrimination in knowing what to discard.

Needing a librettist for this new opera commission, I approached the poet Hugh Maxton, who, I am delighted to say, is in the audience tonight. By way of response, he offered me several outlines for original plots and a summary of *The Words Upon the Window-Pane*. Having twice produced and, on another occasion acted in the play, Hugh Maxton was well acquainted with the passionate intensity of thought and expression which imbues the work. For my part I was instantly struck by the inherent musical possibilities, especially in the role of Mrs Henderson, and I requested Hugh to begin work immediately on creating the libretto.

Yeats wrote the play at Coole Park in 1930, and dedicated it to Lady Gregory. The first performance took place later that year in the Abbey Theatre. The work takes approximately an hour in performance, so a considerable number of modifications were required to create the libretto for the chamber opera. These were partly to meet the terms of the commission, but equally importantly to create the concentration of text and dramatic line, necessitated by a twenty minute chamber opera. The libretto goes directly to the dramatic core of the play, eliminating all sub plots and discursive dialogue. The original seven characters are reduced to five, some of their lines amalgamated and Miss Mackenna, secretary of the Dublin Spiritualists Association becomes Miss LeFanu in the opera.

In the introduction to the published version of the play, Yeats writes, 'Swift haunts me; he is always just around the next corner.' Though he never actually appears in the play, *The Words Upon the Window-Pane* is also haunted and dominated by Jonathan Swift or at least by his turbulent spirit. The play is centred on Swift's complex relationships with Esther Johnson, better known as Stella, and Hester Vanhomrigh, whom Swift furnished with the nickname Vanessa. Swift first met Stella in 1689 at Moor Park, the home of Sir William Temple in Surrey, when she was only eight years of age. Initially acting as her tutor, Swift later brought her to Ireland with him in 1702 and the two maintained a close but somewhat ambiguous relationship. Rumours claiming that they were lovers abounded. It was even maintained that they were secretly married in 1716, though it is hard to know how that would have benefited either of them.

Swift certainly displayed a warmth and tenderness towards Stella that is nowhere else in evidence, either in his writings or in anecdotal commentary. This affection is unambiguously reflected in the libretto:

> Beloved Stella have I wronged you?
> You have no children, no lover, no husband,
> A cross and aging man for friend.
> But do not answer,
> You have answered already in that noble poem you wrote for
> me.

Here, Swift quotes from the poem that Stella wrote in 1721 for his fifty fourth birthday, the words of which are etched upon the window pane of the lodging house room, where the play and opera are set.

> You taught how I might youth prolong,
> By knowing what is right and wrong;
> How from my eyes to bring supplies
> Of lustre to my fading eyes

He continues:

> Because you know I am afraid of ... outliving my friends – and myself – you ... over praise my moral nature ... Yes, you will close my eyes, Stella. O, you will live long after me, but you will close my eyes, dear Stella.

In actual fact Stella didn't live to close Swift's eyes; she died in 1728 and Swift outlived her by seventeen years.

From 1707 to 1714, Swift spent much of his time in London and wielded considerable political power and influence as part of the inner circle of the Tory Government but with the death of Queen Anne the government fell and its leaders were tried for treason for conducting secret negotiations with France during the War of the Spanish Succession. This accounts for the amazing outburst at the end of the play:

> Five great ministers that were my friends are gone,
> Ten great ministers that were my friends are gone.
> I have not fingers enough to count the great ministers
> that were my friends and that are gone.

It was also during these years that Swift first met Hester Vanhomrigh, who became infatuated with him. This relationship was also rather complex: Swift may well have returned Vanessa's initial affections, only to regret it and attempt to end the connection. His appointment to the Deanery of St. Patrick's Cathedral must have seemed like a reprieve but, shortly after his return to Dublin, Vanessa followed him and ensconced herself in nearby Celbridge. Complications inevitably set in and culminated in a confrontation between Swift and Vanessa. It appears that in 1723 Vanessa wrote to Stella asking why she, Vanessa, and Swift shouldn't marry, if he weren't already married to Stella. Swift took grave exception to the letter, rode down to Celbridge and flinging the letter in her face, departed. Vanessa died within a few weeks at the age of thirty-five. The confrontation is vividly depicted in the play and also features prominently in the opera.

From the libretto:

> How dare you write to her?
> How dare you ask if we were married?
> You sit crouching there
> Did you not hear what I said?
> I found you an ignorant girl
> Without intellect, without moral ambition.

In his final years, Swift's physical and mental condition deteriorated rapidly. His premonition of this state of affairs is reflected in the libretto of the opera. Responding to Vanessa's question as to why they can't marry he says:

> I have something in my blood that no child must inherit. I have constant attacks of dizziness. O God, hear the prayer of Jonathan Swift, that afflicted man and grant that he leave to posterity nothing but his intellect, that came to him from heaven.

The setting for the play and opera is a sparsely furnished room in an eighteenth-century house in Dublin. At that time the house was owned by friends of Stella but it is now a lodging house. The Dublin Spiritualist Society have rented some rooms and are holding a series of séances, conducted by the medium, Mrs Henderson, who has returned from London for that purpose. The participants arrive, amongst them a first-time visitor Robert Corbet, a sceptical young man from Trinity, who happens to be writing his thesis on Swift. He immediately recognizes the words etched upon the window pane.

The musical setting for this opening scene is relatively direct. The instrumental ensemble consisting of flute, clarinet, horn, violin, cello, percussion and piano executes a brief prelude, which is intended to create a mood of uneasy expectation. Miss LeFanu's vocal style is mainly syllabic in contrast to the overtly exuberant mode of Robert Corbet, who becomes greatly excited by the words upon the window-pane. His passion for Swift is reflected in his music: widely spaced intervals, and an elaborately decorated melodic line, a premonition of Swift's own music later in the opera. The instrumental music is not intended as a mere accompaniment to the voices, but rather as an independent commentary, which simultaneously amplifies the emotions inherent in the text.

The overall musical style of the opera might be described as a fusion of classical modernism, expressionism, and somewhere in the shadows, though totally disconnected from its source, the elaborate ornamentation of Irish traditional music.

The other participants in the séance arrive, including the whimsical Cornelius Patterson, a sporty type, whose main interest is greyhound racing and who wants to predict the results. It was with some reluctance that Hugh Maxton and I decided to omit the words in reference to Patterson and Miss LeFanu, 'Miss LeFanu will keep him to herself for some minutes. He gives her tips for Harold's Cross.'[14] These words would surely be unique in operatic libretti!

When all the participants are in place, Mrs Henderson enters and the séance begins. Her efforts in contacting their dead relatives, however, are abruptly interrupted by the turbulent spirit of Jonathan Swift, who seems to take her over and speaks through her. Mrs Henderson now enacts the drama of Swift, Stella and Vanessa, becoming each in turn. This play-within-a-play takes place entirely in the mind of Mrs Henderson and since the story and emotions it depicts are conveyed through the spirit of Swift, the process involves further layers. Stella and Vanessa are now portrayed through the memory and imagination of Swift. In reality this constitutes a play-within-a-play within a play. The world of everyday reality and the world of the supernatural, the world of imagination and of memory are juxtaposed. The single most effective dramatic device in *The Words Upon the Window-Pane* is the manner in which Yeats contrives to make the world of the dead far more real and compelling than the world of the living, who sit around the table. Compared to the striking characterization of Swift, Stella and Vanessa, portrayed through the medium, Mrs Henderson, the other participants in the séance are mere spectral shadows. Even Corbet's bravado is mere youthful exuberance.

This extraordinary scene, reflected through the prism of Mrs Henderson's psychic gifts, depicts the confrontation between Swift and Vanessa. In the opera, the text is considerably condensed; it seems to me that a dozen key words would be sufficient: ignorant, ambition, inherit, attacks, God, prayer, Swift, afflicted, intellect, heaven, alone, enemy. I have highlighted these words within the musical setting by the use of elaborate expressionistic melisma, that is to say using several notes for each syllable of the text: the word prayer for example has no fewer than thirty three notes. This of course greatly elongates the time required and makes for very long phrases, but it draws attention to the key words and emotions. A range of over two octaves is required and the music is often at the extremities of the voice, or suddenly leaps from the low to the higher register. The flamboyant bravura of a sentence such as 'O God hear the prayer of Jonathan Swift, that afflicted man and grant that he leave to posterity nothing but his intellect, that came to him from heaven' is highly elaborate, even when spoken. In the musical setting, the melodic line spirals from the high register to the lowest over fourteen bars and takes almost a minute to perform. The normal pace of the spoken word, or anything approaching it, is abandoned in favour of a form of expression, where the sonority and emotion of the vocal line are at least as important as the actual meaning of the text. I would undoubtedly have attracted the censure of the founding figures of opera for lack of clarity. Here, I am prepared to sacrifice the immediate clarity of text in favour of a heightened form of emotional expression.

Vanessa's response to Swift, also sung by Mrs Henderson, is compressed into a single question: 'Can you face solitude with that mind Jonathan?' The gentle pleading lyricism of her music is in stark contrast to that of Swift.

This scene and the following one, in which Swift's relationship with Stella is recollected, form the fulcrum at the core of the play and the opera. Swift's words to Stella are imbued with a tenderness and concern, which is elsewhere absent. We hear in full Stella's poem to Swift, the words of which are those etched upon the window pane.

'Beloved Stella, have I wronged you? You have no children, no lover, no husband. A cross and ageing man for friend. But do not answer – you have answered already in that noble poem you wrote for me:

> You taught how I might youth prolong
> By knowing what is right or wrong.
>
> How from my heart to bring supplies
> Of lustre for my fading eyes.
>
> Because you know I am afraid of solitude, afraid of outliving
> my friends and myself, you overpraise my moral nature. Yes,
> you will close my eyes, dear Stella. You will live long after me,
> but you will close my eyes, dear Stella.'

Once again, the text is compressed in the libretto to allow for musical considerations. The music has a flowing lyricism, which stands in stark contrast to the previous scene.

Only the first four lines of Stella's poem are quoted, but Swift's own valedictory words, 'But you will close my eyes, dear Stella' are incorporated into the musical argument. This is the closest the music comes to what might be described as a set piece – a traditional opera aria. An operatic aria is somewhat akin to a soliloquy in a play in that it frequently expresses the emotional state and inner thoughts of the character. Like so much else in *The Words Upon the Window-Pane* however, this soliloquy and aria are at least at one remove: it was Swift and Stella who experienced the feelings but Mrs Henderson who expresses them or perhaps not even Mrs Henderson herself, since Swift's spirit has taken her over.

I have attempted to create a wistfully melancholic character in the music by the use of appoggiaturas and suspensions. These are musical devices whereby dissonant notes are sounded and then resolved to more consonant chords. There is nothing new here – these devices were available to Monteverdi as a colouristic effect but here they are the actual material substance of the musical expression.

The séance is deemed a failure and all depart except for Corbet, who holds back at the last minute. He is overwhelmed by what he has seen and heard, but is still sceptical about the spirit world. He prefers to believe that Mrs Henderson is an accomplished actress and scholar, who has created the whole scenario. Their ensuing conversation, however, makes it clear that Mrs Henderson has absolutely no idea who Swift was.

Corbet departs and Mrs Henderson is left alone on stage. She is tired. She goes to make a cup of tea and has clearly returned to being herself. This is one of the few places in the opera where Mrs Henderson actually sings in her own voice. The spirit of Swift seems to have evaporated or has it?

[The score and recording of *The Words Upon the Window-Pane* by John Buckley may be consulted at The Contemporary Music Centre, 19 Fishamble Street, Temple Bar, Dublin 8. info@cmc.ie]

[1] William Butler Yeats, *The Words Upon the Window-Pane*, (Dublin, 1934)

[2] Oliver Taplin, *Greek Tragedy in Action* (London, 1978), 1.

[3] T.S. Eliot, *Selected Essays*:3rd ed. (London, 1951)

[4] *Melisma* is the singing of several notes to a single syllable of text, the result being frequently florid and elaborate.

[5] Paul Cartledge, '"Deep plays": theatre as process in Greek civic life' in *The Cambridge Companion to Greek Tragedy*, ed. P. E. Easterling (Cambridge: Cambridge University Press, 1997), 3.

[6] *Monody* refers to a solo song with accompaniment.

[7] *Counterpoint* is the art of combining several melodic lines simultaneously.

[8] Leslie Orrey, *A Concise History of Opera* (London, 1972), 18-19

[9] A *Toccata* is a virtuoso sounding piece. In *L'Orfeo,* the term is used to signify a fanfare.

[10] Taplin, *Greek Tragedy in Action*, 13

[11] Cf. Charles Osborne, *The Complete Operas of Verdi* (London: Da Capo, 1969), 410.

[12] Ibid., 417

[13] Igor Stravinsky, *Poetics of Music* (New York, 1960), 66.

[14] Harold's Cross is a famous greyhound-racing track in Dublin.

Index

Carysfort Press was formed in the summer of 1998. It receives annual funding from the Arts Council.

The directors believe that drama is playing an ever-increasing role in today's society and that enjoyment of the theatre, both professional and amateur, currently plays a central part in Irish culture.

The Press aims to produce high quality publications which, though written and/or edited by academics, will be made accessible to a general readership. The organisation would also like to provide a forum for critical thinking in the Arts in Ireland, again keeping the needs and interests of the general public in view.

The company publishes contemporary Irish writing for and about the theatre.

Editorial and publishing inquiries to:
Carysfort Press Ltd.,
58 Woodfield,
Scholarstown Road,
Rathfarnham,
Dublin 16,
Republic of Ireland.

T (353 1) 493 7383
F (353 1) 406 9815
E: info@carysfortpress.com
www.carysfortpress.com

HOW TO ORDER

TRADE ORDERS DIRECTLY TO:
Irish Book Distribution
Unit 12, North Park, North Road,
Finglas, Dublin 11.

T: (353 1) 8239580
F: (353 1) 8239599
E: mary@argosybooks.ie
www.argosybooks.ie

INDIVIDUAL ORDERS DIRECTLY TO:
eprint Ltd.
35 Coolmine Industrial Estate,
Blanchardstown, Dublin 15.
T: (353 1) 827 8860
F: (353 1) 827 8804 Order online @
E: books@eprint.ie
www.eprint.ie

FOR SALES IN NORTH AMERICA AND CANADA:
Dufour Editions Inc.,
124 Byers Road,
PO Box 7,
Chester Springs,
PA 19425,
USA

T: 1-610-458-5005
F: 1-610-458-7103

The Theatre of Tom Mac Intyre: 'Strays from the ether'

Eds. Bernadette Sweeney and Marie Kelly

This long overdue anthology captures the soul of Mac Intyre's dramatic canon – its ethereal qualities, its extraordinary diversity, its emphasis on the poetic and on performance – in an extensive range of visual, journalistic and scholarly contributions from writers, theatre practitioners.

ISBN 978-1-904505-46-4 €25

Irish Appropriation Of Greek Tragedy

Brian Arkins

This book presents an analysis of more than 30 plays written by Irish dramatists and poets that are based on the tragedies of Sophocles, Euripides and Aeschylus. These plays proceed from the time of Yeats and Synge through MacNeice and the Longfords on to many of today's leading writers.

ISBN 978-1-904505-47-1 €20

Alive in Time: The Enduring Drama of Tom Murphy

Ed. Christopher Murray

Almost 50 years after he first hit the headlines as Ireland's most challenging playwright, the 'angry young man' of those times Tom Murphy still commands his place at the pinnacle of Irish theatre. Here 17 new essays by prominent critics and academics, with an introduction by Christopher Murray, survey Murphy's dramatic oeuvre in a concerted attempt to define his greatness and enduring appeal, making this book a significant study of a unique genius.

ISBN 978-1-904505-45-7 €25

Performing Violence in Contemporary Ireland

Ed. Lisa Fitzpatrick

This interdisciplinary collection of fifteen new essays by scholars of theatre, Irish studies, music, design and politics explores aspects of the performance of violence in contemporary Ireland. With chapters on the work of playwrights Martin McDonagh, Martin Lynch, Conor McPherson and Gary Mitchell, on Republican commemorations and the 90th anniversary ceremonies for the Battle of the Somme and the Easter Rising, this book aims to contribute to the ongoing international debate on the performance of violence in contemporary societies.

ISBN 978-1-904505-44-0 (2009) €20

Ireland's Economic Crisis - Time to Act. Essays from over 40 leading Irish thinkers at the MacGill Summer School 2009

Eds. Joe Mulholland and Finbarr Bradley

Ireland's economic crisis requires a radical transformation in policymaking. In this volume, political, industrial, academic, trade union and business leaders and commentators tell the story of the Irish economy and its rise and fall. Contributions at Glenties range from policy, vision and context to practical suggestions on how the country can emerge from its crisis.

ISBN 978-1-904505-43-3 (2009) €20

Deviant Acts: Essays on Queer Performance

Ed. David Cregan

This book contains an exciting collection of essays focusing on a variety of alternative performances happening in contemporary Ireland. While it highlights the particular representations of gay and lesbian identity it also brings to light how diversity has always been a part of Irish culture and is, in fact, shaping what it means to be Irish today.

ISBN 978-1-904505-42-6 (2009) €20

Seán Keating in Context: Responses to Culture and Politics in Post-Civil War Ireland

Compiled, edited and introduced by Éimear O'Connor

Irish artist Seán Keating has been judged by his critics as the personification of old-fashioned traditionalist values. This book presents a different view. The story reveals Keating's early determination to attain government support for the visual arts. It also illustrates his socialist leanings, his disappointment with capitalism, and his attitude to cultural snobbery, to art critics, and to the Academy. Given the national and global circumstances nowadays, Keating's critical and wry observations are prophetic – and highly amusing.

ISBN 978-1-904505-41-9 €25

Dialogue of the Ancients of Ireland: A new translation of Acallam na Senorach

Translated with introduction and notes by Maurice Harmon

One of Ireland's greatest collections of stories and poems, The Dialogue of the Ancients of Ireland is a new translation by Maurice Harmon of the 12th century *Acallam na Senorach*. Retold in a refreshing modern idiom, the *Dialogue* is an extraordinary account of journeys to the four provinces by St. Patrick and the pagan Cailte, one of the surviving Fian. Within the frame story are over 200 other stories reflecting many genres – wonder tales, sea journeys, romances, stories of revenge, tales of monsters and magic. The poems are equally varied – lyrics, nature poems, eulogies, prophecies, laments, genealogical poems. After the *Tain Bo Cuailnge*, the *Acallam* is the largest surviving prose work in Old and Middle Irish.

ISBN: 978-1-904505-39-6 (2009) €20

Literary and Cultural Relations between Ireland and Hungary and Central and Eastern Europe

Ed. Maria Kurdi

This lively, informative and incisive collection of essays sheds fascinating new light on the literary interrelations between Ireland, Hungary, Poland, Romania and the Czech Republic. It charts a hitherto under-explored history of the reception of modern Irish culture in Central and Eastern Europe and also investigates how key authors have been translated, performed and adapted. The revealing explorations undertaken in this volume of a wide array of Irish dramatic and literary texts, ranging from *Gulliver's Travels* to *Translations* and *The Pillowman*, tease out the subtly altered nuances that they acquire in a Central European context.

ISBN: 978-1-904505-40-2 (2009) €20

Plays and Controversies: Abbey Theatre Diaries 2000-2005

Ben Barnes

In diaries covering the period of his artistic directorship of the Abbey, Ben Barnes offers a frank, honest, and probing account of a much commented upon and controversial period in the history of the national theatre. These diaries also provide fascinating personal insights into the day-to- day pressures, joys, and frustrations of running one of Ireland's most iconic institutions.

ISBN: 978-1-904505-38-9 (2008) €35

Interactions: Dublin Theatre Festival 1957-2007. Irish Theatrical Diaspora Series: 3

Eds. Nicholas Grene and Patrick Lonergan with Lilian Chambers

For over 50 years the Dublin Theatre Festival has been one of Ireland's most important cultural events, bringing countless new Irish plays to the world stage, while introducing Irish audiences to the most important international theatre companies and artists. Interactions explores and celebrates the achievements of the renowned Festival since 1957 and includes specially commissioned memoirs from past organizers, offering a unique perspective on the controversies and successes that have marked the event's history. An especially valuable feature of the volume, also, is a complete listing of the shows that have appeared at the Festival from 1957 to 2008.

ISBN: 978-1-904505-36-5 €25

The Informer: A play by Tom Murphy based on the novel by Liam O'Flaherty

The Informer, Tom Murphy's stage adaptation of Liam O'Flaherty's novel, was produced in the 1981 Dublin Theatre Festival, directed by the playwright himself, with Liam Neeson in the leading role. The central subject of the play is the quest of a character at the point of emotional and moral breakdown for some source of meaning or identity. In the case of Gypo Nolan, the informer of the title, this involves a nightmarish progress through a Dublin underworld in which he changes from a Judas figure to a scapegoat surrogate for Jesus, taking upon himself the sins of the world. A cinematic style, with flash-back and intercut scenes, is used rather than a conventional theatrical structure to catch the fevered and phantasmagoric progression of Gypo's mind. The language, characteristically for Murphy, mixes graphically colloquial Dublin slang with the haunted intricacies of the central character groping for the meaning of his own actions. The dynamic rhythm of the action builds towards an inevitable but theatrically satisfying tragic catastrophe. ' [The Informer] is, in many ways closer to being an original Murphy play than it is to O'Flaherty...' Fintan O'Toole.

ISBN: 978-1-904505-37-2 (2008) €10

Shifting Scenes: Irish theatre-going 1955-1985

Eds. Nicholas Grene and Chris Morash

Transcript of conversations with John Devitt, academic and reviewer, about his lifelong passion for the theatre. A fascinating and entertaining insight into Dublin theatre over the course of thirty years provided by Devitt's vivid reminiscences and astute observations.

ISBN: 978-1-904505-33-4 (2008) €10

Irish Literature: Feminist Perspectives

Eds. Patricia Coughlan and Tina O'Toole

The collection discusses texts from the early 18th century to the present. A central theme of the book is the need to renegotiate the relations of feminism with nationalism and to transact the potential contest of these two important narratives, each possessing powerful emancipatory force. Irish Literature: Feminist Perspectives contributes incisively to contemporary debates about Irish culture, gender and ideology.

ISBN: 978-1-904505-35-8 (2008) €25

Silenced Voices: Hungarian Plays from Transylvania

Selected and translated by Csilla Bertha and Donald E. Morse

The five plays are wonderfully theatrical, moving fluidly from absurdism to tragedy, and from satire to the darkly comic. Donald Morse and Csilla Bertha's translations capture these qualities perfectly, giving voice to the 'forgotten playwrights of Central Europe'. They also deeply enrich our understanding of the relationship between art, ethics, and politics in Europe.

ISBN: 978-1-904505-34-1 (2008) €25

A Hazardous Melody of Being:
Seóirse Bodley's Song Cycles on the poems of Micheal O'Siadhail

Ed. Lorraine Byrne Bodley

This apograph is the first publication of Bodley's O'Siadhail song cycles and is the first book to explore the composer's lyrical modernity from a number of perspectives. Lorraine Byrne Bodley's insightful introduction describes in detail the development and essence of Bodley's musical thinking, the European influences he absorbed which linger in these cycles, and the importance of his work as a composer of the Irish art song.

ISBN: 978-1-904505-31-0 (2008) €25

Irish Theatre in England: Irish Theatrical Diaspora Series: 2

Eds. Richard Cave and Ben Levitas

Irish theatre in England has frequently illustrated the complex relations between two distinct cultures. How English reviewers and audiences interpret Irish plays is often decidedly different from how the plays were read in performance in Ireland. How certain Irish performers have chosen to be understood in Dublin is not necessarily how audiences in London have perceived their constructed stage personae. Though a collection by diverse authors, the twelve essays in this volume investigate these issues from a variety of perspectives that together chart the trajectory of Irish performance in England from the mid-nineteenth century till today.

ISBN: 978-1-904505-26-6 (2007) €20

Goethe and Anna Amalia: A Forbidden Love?

Ettore Ghibellino, Trans. Dan Farrelly

In this study Ghibellino sets out to show that the platonic relationship between Goethe and Charlotte von Stein – lady-in-waiting to Anna Amalia, the Dowager Duchess of Weimar – was used as part of a cover-up for Goethe's intense and prolonged love relationship with the Duchess Anna Amalia herself. The book attempts to uncover a hitherto closely-kept state secret. Readers convinced by the evidence supporting Ghibellino's hypothesis will see in it one of the very great love stories in European history – to rank with that of Dante and Beatrice, and Petrarch and Laura.

ISBN: 978-1-904505-24-2 €20

Ireland on Stage: Beckett and After

Eds. Hiroko Mikami, Minako Okamuro, Naoko Yagi

The collection focuses primarily on Irish playwrights and their work, both in text and on the stage during the latter half of the twentieth century. The central figure is Samuel Beckett, but the contributors freely draw on Beckett and his work provides a springboard to discuss contemporary playwrights such as Brian Friel, Frank McGuinness, Marina Carr and Conor McPherson amongst others. Contributors include: Anthony Roche, Hiroko Mikami, Naoko Yagi, Cathy Leeney, Joseph Long, Noreem Doody, Minako Okamuro, Christopher Murray, Futoshi Sakauchi and Declan Kiberd

ISBN: 978-1-904505-23-5 (2007) €20

'Echoes Down the Corridor': Irish Theatre - Past, Present and Future

Eds. Patrick Lonergan and Riana O'Dwyer

This collection of fourteen new essays explores Irish theatre from exciting new perspectives. How has Irish theatre been received internationally - and, as the country becomes more multicultural, how will international theatre influence the development of drama in Ireland? These and many other important questions.

ISBN: 978-1-904505-25-9 (2007) €20

Musics of Belonging: The Poetry of Micheal O'Siadhail

Eds. Marc Caball & David F. Ford

An overall account is given of O'Siadhail's life, his work and the reception of his poetry so far. There are close readings of some poems, analyses of his artistry in matching diverse content with both classical and innovative forms, and studies of recurrent themes such as love, death, language, music, and the shifts of modern life.

ISBN: 978-1-904505-22-8 (2007) €25 (Paperback)
ISBN: 978-1-904505-21-1 (2007) €50 (Casebound)

Brian Friel's Dramatic Artistry: 'The Work has Value'

Eds. Donald E. Morse, Csilla Bertha and Maria Kurdi

Brian Friel's Dramatic Artistry presents a refreshingly broad range of voices: new work from some of the leading English-speaking authorities on Friel, and fascinating essays from scholars in Germany, Italy, Portugal, and Hungary. This book will deepen our knowledge and enjoyment of Friel's work.

ISBN: 978-1-904505-17-4 (2006) €30

The Theatre of Martin McDonagh: 'A World of Savage Stories'

Eds. Lilian Chambers and Eamonn Jordan

The book is a vital response to the many challenges set by McDonagh for those involved in the production and reception of his work. Critics and commentators from around the world offer a diverse range of often provocative approaches. What is not surprising is the focus and commitment of the engagement, given the controversial and stimulating nature of the work.

ISBN: 978-1-904505-19-8 (2006) €35

Edna O'Brien: New Critical Perspectives

Eds. Kathryn Laing, Sinead Mooney and Maureen O'Connor

The essays collected here illustrate some of the range, complexity, and interest of Edna O'Brien as a fiction writer and dramatist. They will contribute to a broader appreciation of her work and to an evolution of new critical approaches, as well as igniting more interest in the many unexplored areas of her considerable oeuvre.

ISBN: 978-1-904505-20-4 (2006) €20

Irish Theatre on Tour

Eds. Nicholas Grene and Chris Morash

'Touring has been at the strategic heart of Druid's artistic policy since the early eighties. Everyone has the right to see professional theatre in their own communities. Irish theatre on tour is a crucial part of Irish theatre as a whole'. Garry Hynes

ISBN 978-1-904505-13-6 (2005) €20

Poems 2000-2005 by Hugh Maxton

Poems 2000-2005 is a transitional collection written while the author – also known to be W.J. Mc Cormack, literary historian – was in the process of moving back from London to settle in rural Ireland.

ISBN 978-1-904505-12-9 (2005) €10

Synge: A Celebration

Ed. Colm Tóibín

A collection of essays by some of Ireland's most creative writers on the work of John Millington Synge, featuring Sebastian Barry, Marina Carr, Anthony Cronin, Roddy Doyle, Anne Enright, Hugo Hamilton, Joseph O'Connor, Mary O'Malley, Fintan O'Toole, Colm Toibin, Vincent Woods.

ISBN 978-1-904505-14-3 (2005) €15

East of Eden: New Romanian Plays

Ed. Andrei Marinescu

Four of the most promising Romanian playwrights, young and very young, are in this collection, each one with a specific way of seeing the Romanian reality, each one with a style of communicating an articulated artistic vision of the society we are living in. Ion Caramitru, General Director Romanian National Theatre Bucharest.
ISBN 978-1-904505-15-0 (2005) €10

George Fitzmaurice: 'Wild in His Own Way', Biography of an Irish Playwright

Fiona Brennan

'Fiona Brennan's introduction to his considerable output allows us a much greater appreciation and understanding of Fitzmaurice, the one remaining under-celebrated genius of twentieth-century Irish drama'. Conall Morrison

ISBN 978-1-904505-16-7 (2005) €20

Out of History: Essays on the Writings of Sebastian Barry

Ed. Christina Hunt Mahony

The essays address Barry's engagement with the contemporary cultural debate in Ireland and also with issues that inform postcolonial critical theory. The range and selection of contributors has ensured a high level of critical expression and an insightful assessment of Barry and his works.

ISBN: 978-1-904505-18-1 (2005) €20

Three Congregational Masses

Seoirse Bodley

'From the simpler congregational settings in the Mass of Peace and the Mass of Joy to the richer textures of the Mass of Glory, they are immediately attractive and accessible, and with a distinctively Irish melodic quality.' Barra Boydell

ISBN: 978-1-904505-11-2 (2005) €15

Georg Büchner's Woyzeck,

A new translation by Dan Farrelly

The most up-to-date German scholarship of Thomas Michael Mayer and Burghard Dedner has finally made it possible to establish an authentic sequence of scenes. The wide-spread view that this play is a prime example of loose, open theatre is no longer sustainable. Directors and teachers are challenged to "read it again".

ISBN: 978-1-904505-02-0 (2004) €10

Playboys of the Western World: Production Histories

Ed. Adrian Frazier

'The book is remarkably well-focused: half is a series of production histories of Playboy performances through the twentieth century in the UK, Northern Ireland, the USA, and Ireland. The remainder focuses on one contemporary performance, that of Druid Theatre, as directed by Garry Hynes. The various contemporary social issues that are addressed in relation to Synge's play and this performance of it give the volume an additional interest: it shows how the arts matter.' Kevin Barry

ISBN: 978-1-904505-06-8 (2004)   €20

The Power of Laughter: Comedy and Contemporary Irish Theatre

Ed. Eric Weitz

The collection draws on a wide range of perspectives and voices including critics, playwrights, directors and performers. The result is a series of fascinating and provocative debates about the myriad functions of comedy in contemporary Irish theatre. Anna McMullan

As Stan Laurel said, 'it takes only an onion to cry. Peel it and weep. Comedy is harder'. 'These essays listen to the power of laughter. They hear the tough heart of Irish theatre – hard and wicked and funny'. Frank McGuinness

ISBN: 978-1-904505-05-1 (2004)   €20

Sacred Play: Soul-Journeys in contemporary Irish Theatre

Anne F. O'Reilly

'Theatre as a space or container for sacred play allows audiences to glimpse mystery and to experience transformation. This book charts how Irish playwrights negotiate the labyrinth of the Irish soul and shows how their plays contribute to a poetics of Irish culture that enables a new imagining. Playwrights discussed are: McGuinness, Murphy, Friel, Le Marquand Hartigan, Burke Brogan, Harding, Meehan, Carr, Parker, Devlin, and Barry.'

ISBN: 978-1-904505-07-5 (2004)   €25

The Irish Harp Book

Sheila Larchet Cuthbert

This is a facsimile of the edition originally published by Mercier Press in 1993. There is a new preface by Sheila Larchet Cuthbert, and the biographical material has been updated. It is a collection of studies and exercises for the use of teachers and pupils of the Irish harp.
ISBN: 978-1-904505-08-2 (2004)   €35

The Drunkard

Tom Murphy

'The Drunkard is a wonderfully eloquent play. Murphy's ear is finely attuned to the glories and absurdities of melodramatic exclamation, and even while he is wringing out its ludicrous overstatement, he is also making it sing.' The Irish Times

ISBN: 978-1-90 05-09-9 (2004) €10

Goethe: Musical Poet, Musical Catalyst

Ed. Lorraine Byrne

'Goethe was interested in, and acutely aware of, the place of music in human experience generally - and of its particular role in modern culture. Moreover, his own literary work - especially the poetry and Faust - inspired some of the major composers of the European tradition to produce some of their finest works.' Martin Swales

ISBN: 978-1-9045-10-5 (2004) €40

The Theatre of Marina Carr: "Before rules was made"

Eds. Anna McMullan & Cathy Leeney

As the first published collection of articles on the theatre of Marina Carr, this volume explores the world of Carr's theatrical imagination, the place of her plays in contemporary theatre in Ireland and abroad and the significance of her highly individual voice.

ISBN: 978-0-9534257-7-8 (2003) €20

Critical Moments: Fintan O'Toole on Modern Irish Theatre

Eds. Julia Furay & Redmond O'Hanlon

This new book on the work of Fintan O'Toole, the internationally acclaimed theatre critic and cultural commentator, offers percussive analyses and assessments of the major plays and playwrights in the canon of modern Irish theatre. Fearless and provocative in his judgements, O'Toole is essential reading for anyone interested in criticism or in the current state of Irish theatre.

ISBN: 978-1-904505-03-7 (2003) €20

Goethe and Schubert: Across the Divide

Eds. Lorraine Byrne & Dan Farrelly

Proceedings of the International Conference, 'Goethe and Schubert in Perspective and Performance', Trinity College Dublin, 2003. This volume includes essays by leading scholars – Barkhoff, Boyle, Byrne, Canisius, Dürr, Fischer, Hill, Kramer, Lamport, Lund, Meikle, Newbould, Norman McKay, White, Whitton, Wright, Youens – on Goethe's musicality and his relationship to Schubert; Schubert's contribution to sacred music and the Lied and his setting of Goethe's Singspiel, Claudine. A companion volume of this Singspiel (with piano reduction and English translation) is also available.

ISBN: 978-1-904505-04-4 (2003)   €25

Goethe's Singspiel, 'Claudine von Villa Bella'

Set by Franz Schubert

Goethe's Singspiel in three acts was set to music by Schubert in 1815. Only Act One of Schuberts's Claudine score is extant. The present volume makes Act One available for performance in English and German. It comprises both a piano reduction by Lorraine Byrne of the original Schubert orchestral score and a bilingual text translated for the modern stage by Dan Farrelly. This is a tale, wittily told, of lovers and vagabonds, romance, reconciliation, and resolution of family conflict.

ISBN: 978-0-9544290-0-3 (2002)   €20

Theatre of Sound, Radio and the Dramatic Imagination

Dermot Rattigan

An innovative study of the challenges that radio drama poses to the creative imagination of the writer, the production team, and the listener.
"A remarkably fine study of radio drama – everywhere informed by the writer's professional experience of such drama in the making…A new theoretical and analytical approach – informative, illuminating and at all times readable." Richard Allen Cave

ISBN: 978- 0-9534-257-5-4 (2002)   €20

Talking about Tom Murphy

Ed. Nicholas Grene

Talking About Tom Murphy is shaped around the six plays in the landmark Abbey Theatre Murphy Season of 2001, assembling some of the best-known commentators on his work: Fintan O'Toole, Chris Morash, Lionel Pilkington, Alexandra Poulain, Shaun Richards, Nicholas Grene and Declan Kiberd.

ISBN: 978-0-9534-257-9-2 (2002)   €15

Hamlet: The Shakespearean Director

Mike Wilcock

"This study of the Shakespearean director as viewed through various interpretations of HAMLET is a welcome addition to our understanding of how essential it is for a director to have a clear vision of a great play. It is an important study from which all of us who love Shakespeare and who understand the importance of continuing contemporary exploration may gain new insights." From the Foreword, by Joe Dowling, Artistic Director, The Guthrie Theater, Minneapolis, MN

ISBN: 978-1-904505-00-6 (2002) €20

The Theatre of Frank Mc Guinness: Stages of Mutability

Ed. Helen Lojek

The first edited collection of essays about internationally renowned Irish playwright Frank McGuinness focuses on both performance and text. Interpreters come to diverse conclusions, creating a vigorous dialogue that enriches understanding and reflects a strong consensus about the value of McGuinness's complex work.

ISBN: 978-1904505-01-3. (2002) €20

Theatre Talk: Voices of Irish Theatre Practitioners

Eds Lilian Chambers, Ger Fitzgibbon and Eamonn Jordan

"This book is the right approach - asking practitioners what they feel." Sebastian Barry, Playwright "... an invaluable and informative collection of interviews with those who make and shape the landscape of Irish Theatre." Ben Barnes, Artistic Director of the Abbey Theatre

ISBN: 978-0-9534-257-6-1 (2001) €20

In Search of the South African Iphigenie

Erika von Wietersheim and Dan Farrelly

Discussions of Goethe's "Iphigenie auf Tauris" (Under the Curse) as relevant to women's issues in modern South Africa: women in family and public life; the force of women's spirituality; experience of personal relationships; attitudes to parents and ancestors; involvement with religion.

ISBN: 978-0-9534257-8-5 (2001) €10

'The Starving' and 'October Song':

Two contemporary Irish plays by Andrew Hinds

The Starving, set during and after the siege of Derry in 1689, is a moving and engrossing drama of the emotional journey of two men.

October Song, a superbly written family drama set in real time in pre-ceasefire Derry.

ISBN: 978-0-9534-257-4-7 (2001) €10

Seen and Heard: Six new plays by Irish women

Ed. Cathy Leeney

A rich and funny, moving and theatrically exciting collection of plays by Mary Elizabeth Burke-Kennedy, Síofra Campbell, Emma Donoghue, Anne Le Marquand Hartigan, Michelle Read and Dolores Walshe.

ISBN: 978-0-9534-257-3-0 (2001) €20

Theatre Stuff: Critical essays on contemporary Irish theatre

Ed. Eamonn Jordan

Best selling essays on the successes and debates of contemporary Irish theatre at home and abroad. Contributors include: Thomas Kilroy, Declan Hughes, Anna McMullan, Declan Kiberd, Deirdre Mulrooney, Fintan O'Toole, Christopher Murray, Caoimhe McAvinchey and Terry Eagleton.

ISBN: 978-0-9534-2571-1-6 (2000) €20

Under the Curse. Goethe's "Iphigenie Auf Tauris", A New Version

Dan Farrelly

The Greek myth of Iphigenie grappling with the curse on the house of Atreus is brought vividly to life. This version is currently being used in Johannesburg to explore problems of ancestry, religion, and Black African women's spirituality.

ISBN: 978-09534-257-8-5 (2000) €10

Urfaust, A New Version of Goethe's early "Faust" in Brechtian Mode

Dan Farrelly

This version is based on Brecht's irreverent and daring re-interpretation of the German classic. "Urfaust is a kind of well-spring for German theatre… The love-story is the most daring and the most profound in German dramatic literature." Brecht

ISBN: 978-0-9534-257-0-9 (1998)   €20